19.00p
80p

Picturing Learning

Artists & Writers in the Classroom

KAREN ERNST

HEINEMANN
Portsmouth, NH

Heinemann
A division of Reed Publishing (USA) Inc.
361 Hanover Street   Portsmouth, NH 03801–3912
Offices and agents throughout the world

We would like to thank the children and parents who have given their permission to include material in this book. Every effort has been made to contact the copyright holders for permission to reprint borrowed material where necessary. We regret any oversights that may have occurred and would be happy to rectify them in future printings of this work.

Credits for previously published material are on page iv.

Library of Congress Cataloging-in-Publication Data

Ernst, Karen.
    Picturing learning : artists and writers in the classroom / Karen Ernst.
        p.   cm.
    Includes bibliographical references.
    ISBN 0-435-08795-9
    1. Ernst, Karen—Contributions in art teaching.   2. Art—Study and teaching (Elementary)—United States.
    3. Learning by discovery.   4. Visual perception in children.
    5. Group work in educaton.
    I.   Title.
    N89.2.E75A35   1993
    372.5'044—dc20   93-5426
                                                                CIP

Acquisitions editor: Toby Gordon
Production editor: Alan Huisman
Designer: Joni Doherty
Cover illustration by Shirley Xavier
Printed in the United States of America on acid-free paper
97 96 95 94 93 EB 1 2 3 4 5 6 7 8 9 10

For Mom,
who believed in me,
for my many students
who inspired me,
and for Augie,
who encouraged me
to keep going

Contents

Contents

Foreword

DONALD M. MURRAY

When I ask a child to show me writing, I'm as likely to be given a drawing as a draft. Children know what writers know: we write what we see. The relationship of seeing and telling, drawing and writing, is intimate, essential, and a significant aspect of teaching and researching the writing act.

Yet the education profession builds walls where there should be none, isolating instructors and students of visual arts from instructors and students of language arts. We all lose when education locks us into subject-tight compartments.

These walls were torn down for Karen Ernst not on purpose, not by curriculum reform, not by imaginative school management, not for a research project, but because of a budget crisis. Karen, who had been an eighth-grade language arts and social studies teacher for twenty-two years, had that job eliminated; but since she was also certified as an art teacher, she was assigned to teach art to 365 children, kindergarten through fourth grade.

She was terrified. She had never taught at that level, had never taught so many students, had never taught art. She did, however, bring to this new teaching challenge a lifelong interest in art, the habit of sketching, and experience in the teaching of writing. The result was the best kind of classroom-centered research, in which the students instruct the teacher.

Karen has a disciplined research eye combined with the down-to-earth vision of the experienced classroom teacher. This is not a look-at-what-my-wonderful-children-are-doing book. Karen creates the situation in clear prose and authoritative sketches, explains what she did and why, and then allows her students' words and drawings to document what happened. She treats the students with respect, and they show how much they deserve her respect as they talk as artists who are using their explored craft to perform the mission of the artist: to record, explore, and celebrate the world with line or word, color or story. (I add here that the book is also about reading. Karen taught her students to read art by the masters and to read the art emerging from their own hands.)

This book, which began life as a doctoral dissertation, will instruct and inspire teachers of all subjects at all levels; but it should be required reading for every visual arts and language arts teacher, and every music and drama teacher as well. It should inspire curriculum reform to destroy the artificial walls between the art studio and the writers workshop.

This book should also stimulate a new body of research into how artists and writers—student and professional—see, record, and explore their world through line, written and drawn. I think this cross-discipline research could provide major breakthroughs in the disciplines of both art and writing.

The author continually demonstrates the good drawing and the good writing she is trying to teach. There is no jargon here, no inflated diction, just the honest, direct testimony of a teacher in the classroom, creating an environment in which children can teach themselves—and all of us who read this important work.

Acknowledgments

Over the last few years my work has followed what seemed a meandering path, similar to the contour line of my drawings. That path has connected me with many people who have contributed to the ongoing story, who have supported and encouraged me, who have helped form the final picture.

My many students—those in my eighth-grade classrooms, those who kept returning, and later my new, younger students—were always willing and eager participants in my inquiry. They began to wonder with me about the role of the arts in learning and were open to expressions, feelings, and my questions. As my former students returned to share their memories, they informed me of the importance of my work. Their responses propelled me. I thank each one for participating with me as young colleagues.

Also at school, I thank Angela Wormser-Reid and the teachers and parents at Kings Highway for opening their doors to collaboration, for giving me freedom to create, and for teaching me about teaching young children—not with prescription, but with saying back to me what was working, what they noticed, and what they thought stood out in the artists workshop. Thank you, Kings Highway, for being my ongoing peer conference group.

In my search for members of my doctoral committee I am grateful my path crossed with that of each member. Ruth Hubbard and I seemed to speak the same language— of art and writing. She helped me see the significance of the layers of meaning in my work, she shared an excitement for my mountain of data, and she questioned and pushed me to rewrite, to retell, while she assured me I could make it clearer. Maxine Greene's eloquent and powerful words about the role of the arts in education inspired me to attempt to translate her philosophy into my classroom experience. I also thank Mary Sheerin, Roni Natov, June Gould, and Mariagnese Cattaneo for the support and knowledge they held as beacons on my path.

My writing group, Community of Writers (COWs), June Gould, Maxine Greene, Maureen Miletta, and Kathleen Reilly, listened to my story and helped me write it as they listened to drafts of thoughts, looked at the whole picture, connected my story to the stories of education. A special thanks to Kathleen Reilly for her hours of help in reading and editing the final manuscript and to Maureen Miletta and Brenda Power for proofreading it.

No line in the picture is incidental; each leads to the final product. Thanks to the audience of teachers who helped me see how my story affected their own stories of teaching. Thanks to Thomas Newkirk, to Donald Murray, and to Toby Gordon at Heinemann for their interest and their role in helping me understand the bigger picture of my work.

The boldness of my line comes from a confidence that is a result of my support at home. My life with Augusto da Silva and his family is embedded in every stroke of my pen. Through his support, encouragement, and deep belief in children and education, he helped me to keep going. A builder by profession, his strength provides the foundation for my line, for my story, for my picturing learning.

P*rologue*

I draw in contour line. My contour drawings throughout this book work with words to tell my story of an artists workshop. As I look at a person or object I pretend that my pen is touching it, and I begin to follow the line of the subject, letting my pen move along the edge, outlining the silhouette, going into the folds of the shirt, the wisps of hair, the hands crossed on the table. Contour drawings have a three-dimensional quality; they show thickness and depth. When I draw I try not to look at my paper. I use the drawing to help me notice first, then look closer, to move inside where my experience is. As my pen makes squiggly lines for hair, dives into the knee, and marks a line that defines a hand, I see and begin to understand the object I am drawing. My mind leaps to words to record what I hear, what I am thinking, or what I am questioning. In *The Natural Way to Draw*, Kimon Nicolaides writes, "A contour study is not a thing that can be finished. It is having a particular experience, which can continue as long as you have the patience to look" (p. 11). Contour drawing is a journey for me, going from the outside to the innermost place in my mind. Some find contour drawing intimidating: they fear that their line may go off the edge of the page.

As an experienced English teacher in a new position as art teacher in an elementary school, I used drawing and writing to chart a course of discovery for me and my students. I came to this new assignment with confidence in myself as a classroom teacher. I believed in learning as a process; I knew how to run a writers workshop; I learned in collaboration with my students. Classroom research was what took me inside the real thinking and meaning-making actions of my students in the classroom community. Although I did not know where I was going as an art teacher, I was not afraid to "go off the edge of the page." I knew that my research, recorded in drawing and writing, would lead to a series of pictures. As with contour drawings, the outcome of my research was not clear, but I trusted the method and my meandering line.

It was the risk of my journey, of my drawings, coupled with my constant written reflections that helped me find the ideas for artists notebooks and the parallel to my eighth-grade writers workshop. A collage tells the story of this journey; it is the metaphor that holds the pieces of my perceptions, the memories of my eighth graders, and the stories of my new students' learning. As in any journey, there were surprises and echoes of past experience. I think of Maxine Greene, who wrote in *The Dialectic of Freedom:*

> From a human perspective, that of a teacher beginning a school year, a writer beginning a book, a child beginning the first grade, nothing is fully predictable or determined. All kinds of things are possible, although none can be guaranteed. When risks are taken, when people do indeed act on their freedom, a kind of miracle has taken place. Arendt reminds us that we ourselves are the authors of such miracles, because it is we who perform them—and we who have the capacity to establish a reality of our own. (p. 56)

I took myself and my experiences to my new classroom, and I invented a space for learning.

I began in September 1989, and I filled twenty-two research journals with narratives and drawings of my students. These are the shards and fragments that mark the phases of this journey; the meaning is held in the continuum of the line of the drawings and the words. Each drawing and reflection led to invention, to change, to taking action, and to a deeper understanding of the classroom.

Picturing Learning, then, describes this journey. Nicolaides writes, "Seeing depends on knowing. Knowing comes from a constant effort to encompass reality with all of your senses, all that is you" (p. 221). What I saw, drew, and recorded in this classroom was based on who I am, what I know as a teacher. I want you, my readers, to be there as I discover and learn. Through my words and pictures, you will come to your own understanding, will take the continuous line of this story into your own. "There is always a bigger truth undiscovered—unsaid—uncharted until you meet it," Nicolaides asserts (p. 221). It was so as I began picturing learning.

"Every child is an artist. The problem is how to remain an artist once he/she grows up."

PABLO PICASSO

1
Overlapping Pieces

My dark brown braids, looped up and tied with red bows, seemed suspended as I leaned over, drawing my picture. In making a red house with a shiny blue roof, I pressed so hard with my crayons I could feel the coloring bump rise on my middle finger. Miss Schneider, my kindergarten teacher, stood behind me admiring my drawing, and as the other students pushed away from the table, cleaned up their materials, and prepared to go to story time, Miss Schneider allowed me to finish the red house with the blue roof. It was then I knew I wanted to be an artist.

The day was hot and steamy, often the case on first days of school. "Meet me on the rug by the red house for a story" was printed on the easel by the door, directions for the first classes as they entered the artists workshop. The red house, painted on a big, white banner hanging on the back wall of my new classroom, was like the picture I had colored as a kindergartner. Under the red house was a quote by Pablo Picasso: "Every child is an artist. The problem is how to remain an artist once he [or she] grows up."

My new classroom, in my new school, was ready for my 365 students, kindergarten through fourth grade. My first year as an art teacher was also my twenty-second year of teaching. I had always taught eighth graders social studies and language arts, and I was certified in art. As a result of declining enrollment and low seniority, I was assigned to this new position. During this first year I was teacher, learner, participant-observer, artist, and writer with my new students as I set out to create an artists workshop, a community of learning where reading, writing, and picture making worked together to help students learn, think, express themselves, and make meaning.

This is the story of that workshop, which was created through a collage of words and pictures of my learning and, most important, that of my co-learners, my students. Robert Motherwell, a master of collage, wrote that this medium is a type of private diary, one that incorporates personal memory. The collage that is this book includes memories of my emergence as an art teacher with a history of teaching in a writing-process classroom; my work as a researcher, where I used drawing and writing as tools for observing and understanding my students at work; and the stories of children's learning. It also includes the words and pictures of my students, beginning with their first pictures made in kindergarten.

From the easel to the signs dangling overhead, my classroom reflected my landscape, my personal history, my work in the twenty-one classrooms before this one. Working as a teacher-researcher had taught me to question my learning and that of my students and helped to change my own practice.

Childhood, Classrooms: Landscapes

My fifteen-by-fifty-foot basement classroom was filled with bright light from curtainless windows, color from posters around the room, green plants, and bins and carts of materials available to the students. Spaces for work were clearly identified by white signs with titles lettered in black: "Gallery"; "Studio." My new classroom revealed my beliefs about teaching and learning, reflected teachers and writers who had influenced my work over the years, paralleled my writers workshop, and aimed toward the artists workshop of my imagination. A white banner splashed with a quote, "Welcome to a place of excellence, a place where we come together as the best we know how to be," welcomed my students as they arrived. I wanted the experience in this classroom to connect to the whole learning of the students, to encourage art as a way of knowing in their emerging literacy.

My teaching had been influenced by the writing-workshop approach of Nancie Atwell, Donald Graves, and Lucy Calkins, where work in the classroom is based on a naturalistic approach to writing, where students select their own topics, confer with peers as well as the teacher about their drafts in process, revise, edit, and publish their work. Skills are learned within the context of the students' own writing, balanced with the guidance of the teacher. The teacher's decisions in the classroom are based on the ongoing work of the students and the teacher's own involvement as a participating writer and learner, not on a plan dictated by an established sequential curriculum. I wanted learning to be a process in my art classroom as well.

In the writing-workshop classroom, students are encouraged to use their writing as a way to understand their thought processes, to make meaning, and to express their ideas; writing is seen as a meaning-making and symbolizing activity. Just as writing led my students into the process of discovery, learning, and making meaning, I wanted creating pictures to do the same. I built upon the ideas of Maxine Greene, Ann Berthoff, and Ruth Hubbard, who had expanded literacy—normally defined as comprehension through reading and writing—to include the visual. Ruth Hubbard (1989), on the complementary processes of drawing and writing, notes, "As each of us attempts our search for meaning, we need a medium through which our ideas can take shape. But there is not just one medium; productive thought uses many ways to find meaning. Our ideas may take form in images, movement, or inner speech" (p. 3).

Traditionally, art classes were confined to making things: sculptures, paintings, crafts. I wanted the focus in the artists workshop to be on thinking, expressing, and making connections between art and the students' whole learning, their emerging literacy in reading and writing. Here pictures as well as language would be part of the continuum of forming—that is, making meaning.

As my students confronted a blank white piece of paper, they would bring to it their experiences, ideas, and thinking; by filling the page with their colors, shapes, and lines, they would discover, express, and name their learning, and move on to further forming. Words and pictures would be used as complementary processes. I wanted to encourage students to let words lead to thinking as they incorporated picture making into the process of learning.

Bold black letters announced the artists workshop. Knowing that my classroom would be my students' first encounter with the workshop approach, I wanted the signs in the classroom to tell the students my assumptions about learning. Painted in bright primary colors, the signs displayed passages from children's literature. Using a passage from *Caretakers of Wonder* by Cooper Edens, I encouraged students to "imagine what you most would like to do to help keep the world magical." I wanted imagination to play an important part in our workshop. Byrd Baylor, author of *When Clay Sings*, helped me express my commitment to honor individual differences when she wrote, "Every piece of clay is a piece of someone's voice... and sings its own way." A quotation from poet and artist Antoine de Saint-Exupéry, "It is impossible to live without poetry and color and love," suggested my belief that drawing and writing are complementary and that the aim of the workshop is to create a community where students would collaborate and learn together. Another Baylor quote, from *I'm in Charge of Celebrations*, stated, "I keep a notebook and I write the date and then I write about the celebration," reflecting my philosophy that writing is a way of thinking and discovering—the reason why I was including writing in the artists workshop. Keeping their own notebooks would help students see their writing as complementary to their drawing, and would help them construct and extend the experience beyond the picture.

I left the door to the outside open, hoping a breeze would cool the tensions of the first day. I planned to leave that door open, weather permitting, to be a reminder that this classroom, and the students' words and pictures, could lead to an awareness of the world around us, what Maxine Greene calls "wide-awakeness." I wanted this art class to be connected to whole learning and to encourage the use of imagination. My eyes scanned the room from the open door to the sharing area. It was there that most classes would begin, the students looking at art, discussing art, listening to stories, interpreting their pictures, and learning to talk about what they noticed and perceived. They would see and hear possibilities that would feed into their own work. During this year the work in art was to be two dimensional; students would paint, draw, make collages, and write. The routine enabled the students to predict their process in their weekly art experience and freed them to come up with their own creative projects. My "Permissions" sign (see margin), which I had brought from my eighth-grade classroom, hung over the sink, reminding me as much as my new, younger students, that "it is OK to try something you don't know." (All the statements on the chart are from Wiseman's book *Making Things*.)

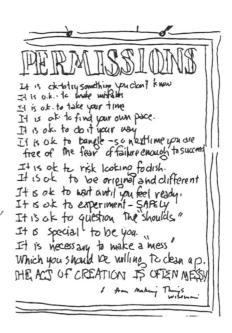

Linda, crippled from childhood with arthritis, sat in the Author's Chair in my eighth-grade classroom, reading her personal narrative about the disease she had lived with for a lifetime. Her presence and her voice were powerful for her audience of peers and teacher. I thought back to the day this shy, thoughtful eighth grader broke her silence at last when she shared her writing with us after our five-minute writing warm-up. After listening to her story we wrote notes to her about the gift we received through lis-

Just Torn-Paper Stories

tening. Her risk taking in our community gave us strength; we returned that gift with encouragement to keep going. Care in building a community allowed students to take risks.

Geoff always wrote straightforward, restrained pieces about a football game, his sneakers, his friends. I was discouraged by the lack of expression, descriptive language, and apparent feeling in his work. In early spring Geoff entered the classroom and announced: "I have written something, but it doesn't sound like me."

We learned that he had discovered a voice he'd never heard before when he wrote about going to his grandparents' farm, a piece full of pictures created by his use of language. He reminded me that students learned at their own pace, learned from each other, and that I had to be willing to wait for breakthroughs in learning to occur.

Coming into this new classroom, I wanted to retain the spirit of my former literate communities, and my roles as teacher, facilitator, reader, writer, and learner that I had experienced in my eighth-grade writers workshop. The stories of Geoff, the memory of listening to Linda read, and the feeling I had as a teacher sitting in the eighth graders' circle of writers were what drove me to shape the artists workshop with the same ingredients and surprise. With the arrival of the first of my seventeen new classes, my learning began.

Standing at the door of the artists workshop, wearing a blue smock with "Miss Ernst" printed on the pocket and a heart drawn on the sleeve, I invited the children to enter, asking each one to read the directions on the easel every time they arrived. Despite my nervousness I remembered the importance of establishing routines from the beginning. I watched the line of little persons spread into the room. Anxious about beginning, I forced myself to allow time for the children to let their eyes wander, to read the landscape. They passed through the Writing Center, an area with one round table for private work. I had printed the date, September 6, 1989, and a passage written by an artist on the

Wednesday 4

Meet me on the rug.

This room is filled with unknown possibilities. I am ready to begin room #5 and wanting to push toward wide-awareness, open eyed awareness, and consciousness of the possibilities within each artist. I want this to be a workshop —

green chalkboard there. I would eventually quote my students as well as mature artists and published writers. A large Raggedy Ann, a gift from my eighth graders, was propped on a blue file cabinet, the eventual home of the artists notebooks. Paper was stacked on shelves under the windows, and bins of markers, scissors, and crayons were on a rolling cart, available to students. The paint cart stood separately near the Writing Center; the dispensing of paint would require my supervision.

The class settled onto the rug next to the red house, an area labeled "Sharing." I sat in the green chair next to the shelves of children's books and waited while my students' eyes focused on me and the pages of my drawing and writing. My journal showed them who I was. I explained how I used my journal to help me observe and understand; I told them the story of the red house I had made in kindergarten, that I was interested in the stories of the pictures they would make while in this artists workshop. Our community began here on the rug. Here we learned how to look at, think, and talk about art; we had opportunities to consider the work of other students, artists, and writers; and we provided a chance for students to rehearse their own work.

As I asked the children to introduce themselves by saying their name and their favorite color, the voices seemed to crack my silent anxiety.

"Carl, brown."

"Jessica, blue."

"Alice, red."

"Christina, purple."

I was guided by remembering how important it was to hear the voices of my eighth graders on the first days of school.

I wondered if the students sensed my anxiety as I turned the pages of *Mouse Paint*, by E. S. Walsh. We looked together for shape, color, and story while I helped them focus on the beautiful fuzzy edges of the mice and the blobs of color. Throughout the year works by poets, illustrators, and writers would awaken their ideas and imagination and inspire their pictures, not be used as prescriptive story starters or models. Literature and art helped me show the possibility of imagination; techniques in drawing, painting, design; how pictures and words could express feelings and ideas—stories. The works would inspire students in ways I had not yet imagined.

We moved over to the Big Table for a minilesson. This "Big Table" was a wooden table with small lockers underneath that held the portfolios of each student. These portfolios, where students would keep each piece of work they made, would provide a record of their progress over the year.

My new students huddled around me at the table as I suggested that we could achieve a look like the fuzzy edges of the mice through tearing paper. We began with torn-paper collage, a nonthreatening, freeing medium. Tearing a piece of colored paper, I held it up, looked at it, talked about what I was thinking, and what I saw as I created a collage before their eyes. I wanted them to watch me risk and create, to learn technique, all with the intention of building their visual vocabulary, not just as a how-to model. I talked about how to apply the glue, but most important I heard myself begin to tell the story of my picture, about my cat, Pepper. Later in the day I reflected in my journal on the first lesson, my students' and mine: "I knew their pictures were stories. I wondered what they could make from their imagination through tearing. I never called it collage, just torn-paper stories."

Work began quietly in those first meetings of each class in an area I called the Studio, at the other end of the room from the rug and sharing area. A busy, silent seriousness filled the room as Vivaldi's "Four Seasons" delicately echoed throughout. After the students made a name tag for their portfolios (which they would be given at the next class meeting), they began their torn-paper stories, using only glue, paper, and their imagination. I wanted them to

Pictures, Meanings: The First Days of Making

think about "next time," and about art in connection to their learning throughout the week. Four students were seated at each table to encourage collaboration; some slumped on their stools while they worked. Most of the younger students stood next to the stool, propping one leg on it for balance. Nothing seemed to get in the way in these first days of making pictures. On two sides of the Studio was the Gallery, a changing display of art reproductions. The work of artists would inspire and challenge my students as they worked.

At the end of our work, after clean-up time, the students settled back onto their stools. I asked them to face each other as they shared what they had noticed or discovered through their work or in the room that day. The memory of my eighth graders reminded me how much I would learn through asking questions. The voices of my new students, telling me their meanings and discoveries, kept me going as I struggled to understand my new assignment, to know the direction of this emerging workshop. Here, as before, my students would act as my informants in designing the process in the classroom.

"I got the idea from the night and the moon and the sun going down and water and the big waves."

"When I look at my picture I think of my beach. I love the sound of the ocean. That's why I called my picture 'Ocean of the Sound.'"

In the same way that tearing paper led me to a story, these first voices breaking the silence in the first sessions of our workshop led me to understand that their pictures were stories too, with titles, images, sounds, and feelings.

In our next session, we began by looking at two works, one by Picasso, the other by Braque. Students discussed what they saw in the paintings and learned how the artists collaborated on their work. Afterward I pulled pictures from portfolios, lifted the red-house banner like a curtain on a stage, and tacked a few pictures made by the students to the blank board reserved for this sharing. As we looked at their collages (see Figure 1–1 for an example),

VanGogh's sunflowers are a burst of yellow behind Picasso's Guernica.
Braque is leaned on the counter top each — their work shown
together with a hint of The MOMA in my small classroom
gallery. It is layered with postcards and posters, reproductions
from my learning and writing at museums — It is is part
of my guided journey here in the art room. The red bulletin
board sports notes and memos, menus and a calendar
under a hand-painted sign "In the Arts" at school   and
beyond. Will this corner, my investigation connect my students to
the world of art and possibility?

FIGURE 1–1
A student's first collage.

I said, "Let's look, relax, be quiet, let your eyes scan all of the pictures. Think about what you see, what comments you can make." Hands went up, filling the space with their visions.

"This one reminds me of . . ."

"I like the way . . ."

"The colors in this one . . ."

From the very beginning my students showed me that pictures held many meanings.

Even though I had begun with a demonstration, I knew I had to keep moving away from a "do as I do" model to helping students envision their own projects. I began taking a "Status of the Class" (Atwell 1987b, p. 73), calling on each student and, as everyone listened, recording what each was planning to make and the media he or she would use. As in the writers workshop, encouraging student choice was central to the routine of the artists workshop.

we paint what we see . . . not what we know

Preparing for Parents' Night, I mounted our first exhibition on the hallway bulletin boards throughout the school, displaying a collage by each child. Although we had had only a few sessions thus far and many of the collages were more glue than paper (see Figure 1–2), I knew the importance of showing each student's beginning work, honoring the best they knew how to be. Exhibition, analogous to publishing, was a strong motivational and educational force for students and the community of parents and teachers beyond the classroom. Through these torn-paper, cut-paper collages, parents could see our beginning in the artists workshop as we went public that night. The hallways were filled with our ongoing learning, my students' and mine, in our torn-paper stories (see Figure 1–3).

At the beginning of the first day of school that year, as I stood outside on bus duty in the heat of the morning and watched the buses pull up to the curb and open their doors, it all seemed so new to me. The kindergartners,

Drawing the Line: From Research to Practice

FIGURE 1–2
A kindergartner's collage.

FIGURE 1–3
A torn-paper story.

dressed in their first day's finest, stumbled their way down the tall steps of the bus toward their first day of school. I was amazed to see parents lining the driveway and sidewalk, crying, waving, smiling, as they watched this important first day of school begin. In the middle school, it was different: children bounded unchaperoned off the bus and into their own world. The differences and similarities between teaching eighth graders in a writers workshop and elementary students in art were evident from the very first day. I began picturing learning, my students' and my own.

Sitting in the green chair at the end of each day and reflecting in my journal became significant to this emerging workshop. The memory of my first days was blurred by my continuing anxiety and tension, my questions about what to do next. The direction of those first days was held steady by my research journal and by the observations, questions, and recollections of former students. My role as teacher-researcher continued to guide me in this new assignment. Just as the parents' cameras captured their child's first day of school, my research journal helped me begin collecting pictures of learning.

Nothing I had read or experienced told me what to do in many situations in the first weeks. There was Anna, a kindergartner, coming into the room on our first day, walking past the easel, holding her classroom teacher's hand, crying. Between sobs she wailed, "I can't draw." Calmly, her teacher turned Anna over to me, saying, "She does this with all of her special teachers, so I'll just leave." Empathizing with Anna's fear, I held her on my lap while I read *Mouse Paint*. We held on to each other as I turned the pages. Some time later, wanting to collaborate with the classroom teachers, I followed one teacher's suggestion to focus on Halloween. Without knowing their abilities, I set out to have her kindergarten class make pumpkins; I provided the students with orange paper, glue, scissors, and markers. I quickly learned that I had given too many directions and materials at once; their teacher returned at the end of the hour to find what looked like orange snakes spread across the counter. This incident taught me to take one step at a time, to teach technique, to move at the students' pace, to avoid using a ready-made plan without knowing the background of the class.

When I introduced the notion of artists notebooks to a third-grade class, a student asked if he could "just draw" instead of write. I hesitated. My initial reaction, which I know came from the "separation of activities" approach taken by my own teachers, was to say no, he "shouldn't" draw when the activity was writing. But conscious of *my* need to combine the activities and wanting to stay open to the needs of my students in the way each approached the interplay of words and images, I answered yes. I learned about possibility and risk taking, and my students reminded me to be an authentic learner, to remember that I did not know all the answers, but that I was also in the class to discover, record, reflect, and inquire as a teacher-researcher and as an artist.

Once during those first days as I observed students working at their tables, my pen stopped as I saw a kindergartner fall gracefully off her tall stool and almost without effort climb back up and resume her work. That seemed a metaphor for these first meetings of my new classes, in the students' first efforts at making the pictures that would ultimately emerge in our artists workshop. Here my students and I began to discover our voices and palettes, inspired by literature and art, through a process framed by a routine based on the writers workshop—a routine that encouraged collaboration, exhibition, and new ideas.

The story of this year is a collage, a visual metaphor, in which I have pieced together the memories of my work with eighth graders and the stories and pictures of younger students' learning in an emerging artists workshop.

Today the sun is overcoming the clouds. We had rain yesterday and I remet my goals, the Fitzgeralds, and my calm.

2

A Researcher Draws, A Teacher and Artist Questions

METHODOLOGY OF THE
EMERGING WORKSHOP

"Wait until you hear my latest, Miss Ernst."
"Could you read this?"
"Can I have the first conference today?"
As I stood my post in the main hallway while classes switched,
my eighth-grade students greeted me and asked questions as they
anticipated our daily meeting in language arts class. As I met my
students each day and collaborated with other eighth-grade teach-
ers to create the curriculum, I knew the work in our classroom
was at the center of my students' whole learning.

At my new school I was called a "special teacher," a title I found unfamiliar after being an eighth-grade language arts teacher for many years. Art, music, physical education, computer science, and library studies were "the specials" outside, or in addition to, the rest of the curriculum, which was offered in self-contained classes. As I began my experience as an art teacher, memories of my eighth-grade language arts class, of its sense of community, of my relationship with my students spilling into conversations beyond the classroom, propelled my thinking. In the language arts class, I would question my students about their learning and change my classroom practice based on this continuing inquiry. I remembered the class as a commu

Beginning the Line:
The Setting, The Questions,
The Role of Teacher Research

nity of learners engaged in their own excited inquiry about learning, writing, and reading. I was a stranger to the elementary classroom and a stranger to the art curriculum, but no stranger to teacher research, teaching, children, learning, and the arts as a way of making meaning.

This book reflects the emergence of the artists workshop over one school year, a ten-month period from August 1989 through June 1990 in a suburb of New York City. The thirteen first- through fourth-grade classes "had art" one hour a week; the four kindergarten classes had art forty-five minutes a week. Each class ranged from twenty to twenty-five students. The principal, in her fourth year at the school, had attracted many teachers, both experienced and new, because she was clearly interested in the welfare, happiness, and quality of education of each student. The school's positive atmosphere was apparent to me from my first visit. The teachers were generally process oriented, many were involved in whole language practices, and the majority were interested in collaborating with me from the beginning: sharing their curriculum, indicating upcoming plans, welcoming me into their classrooms to observe and learn about students younger than I had yet known in my years of teaching.

Since this school was the feeder school for my former middle school and was located across the playing fields from it, I knew many of the older siblings of my new students. Parents were very involved in the PTA and often participated in classroom activities, and they were enthusiastic about my new position, which I had obtained when the former art teacher retired. Along with the memories of my eighth-grade learning communities, I brought with me definite beliefs in education: that the focus should be on the process, not the product; that writing is a way of thinking and critical to any classroom or discipline; that art is a way of knowing, of making meaning; and that learning from observing students is a way to bring change to classroom practice.

I began with a question: What happens when I translate my experience teaching eighth-grade writers workshop and my experience as an artist into an elementary art classroom? I needed to demystify the dichotomy between teaching middle-school and elementary students. In the process of developing the artists workshop, I constantly stepped back to observe my students in order to define a methodology and my role. Observation provided the details I needed to gain new understanding of my teaching practice. As Bogdan and Biklen put it, "Because teachers acting as researchers not only perform their duties but also watch themselves, they step back and, distanced from immediate conflicts, they are able to gain a larger view of what is happening" (p. 209). As the workshop evolved, my questions changed. Initially, my focus was on me and my methods; later I concentrated on the direction taken by specific classes. Ultimately, my students' learning became the focus of my observations and questions.

At that point, new questions arose: What relationship does a writers workshop have to an artists workshop? How do choice and ownership, exhibition and publishing, immersion in literature and art, fit in? How does collaboration of teacher with students and students with students enhance learning? What happens when writing becomes an integral part of the art experience?

Reflecting on my practice and new learning on a daily basis helped me draw on the experience of my former classrooms and put my findings into practice. Here my work as a researcher guided me. My use of drawing and writing in my research journal was central to my observation of and communication with the students. Drawing was a way for me to take field notes and was an essential part of my teaching and research.

As a language arts teacher, I knew my subject was an integral part of my students' everyday learning, but as a special teacher I wondered how I could make art part of the students' whole learning as well. By describing my role as a researcher and sharing what I learned in the development of the artists workshop, I invite other teacher-researchers to make similar inquiries about their own teaching.

Opening Doors: The Collaborative Nature of the Research

artist's smock

The doors to the artists workshop opened into the school and out to the community. Parents often peeked in, entered to talk about their children or to watch an art class, or just waved as they passed by in the parking lot. My intention was to establish this "special class" as part of a learning community, including children, teachers, and parents, and to draw upon that community to learn about teaching younger children. Informing the school community about our emerging workshop and collaborating with teachers was key in helping make the arts part of the whole curriculum.

Educational researchers have emphasized the importance of collaboration, that all participants see themselves as members of a learning community. This perspective has value for both teachers and students. The collaborative aspects of my work—observing other classrooms, telling parents about the workshop process, and supporting other teachers in their own classroom inquiries—were layers that informed my pedagogy.

"What's the art teacher doing up here?" a kindergartner called out as I settled into the corner of his classroom to observe, take notes on the class's activities, and make connections to our work in the artists workshop. As I watched these kindergartners work in groups, I drew one little boy at the easel, the rolled-up sleeves of his smock falling down over his wrists. I noticed other children taking tags from an activity board, placing their name tag next to an activity, and moving to that area. Some were coloring and cutting dragon pieces; others were making bears that were characters in stories they had been read; still others were playing with blocks or working in the science corner.

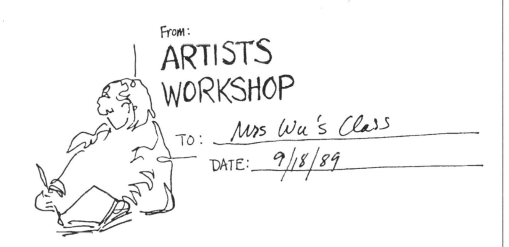

From:
ARTISTS WORKSHOP

TO: _Mrs Wu's Class_

DATE: _9/18/89_

I enjoyed visiting your class for a few minutes today. It's the way I get ideas for our work in art. It looks like you have a wonderful start on stories. We can make pictures to go along with them.

MissErnst

I realized that the group was able to do a variety of activities at once.

In a second-grade classroom I watched a familiar activity, writers workshop. As the teacher conferred with students, one student worked alone on his writing, others discussed their work while sitting on bean bags on the floor, and still others worked together at tables. Observing in these classrooms helped assure me that my younger students could benefit from a workshop approach and that I could collaborate with them. It was in other teachers' classrooms that I learned how to better focus on the students' real world of learning and not on an art curriculum unconnected to their needs. This insight helped me define the artists workshop and my role.

My visits were always followed by a letter from the artists workshop. "I enjoyed visiting your class for a few minutes today," a typical note might begin. I frequently wrote notes following an art class as well. Classroom teachers read these notes to the class and then posted them on the board. My notes reminded students to think about their next project, responded to their performance in art class, or reported on what I had observed. These notes from the artists workshop helped to make art part of the conversation in the regular classrooms and encouraged students to think about art during their week-long absence from the art room. The hundred or so notes I wrote throughout the year provided a chronology of my written connection with the students.

Often, classroom teachers would come into the artists workshop to observe. One teacher stood in back, observing his class of fourth graders as they worked on their pictures; he then moved throughout the room reading the artists notebooks. Another teacher sat on the perimeter of the rug in the sharing area, listening to her third graders discuss the student paintings pinned to the board. The music teacher collaborated with me on school assemblies, incorporating students' pictures and writing as part of the program. Classroom teachers worked with me as we prepared for performances, aesthetic activities, and museum field trips. About half of the teachers stayed for the beginning of art class or came early to pick up the students and listen to our end-of-class sharing. An informed community, teachers and parents, opened the door to my further learning, thus benefitting my classroom and my inquiry.

Mothers would stand in the main hallway, examining the pictures in the all-school exhibition and reading the wall texts about the process of learning in the art room. The exhibition showed parents the process and products of learning in the workshop, gained their support, and encouraged their questioning and response. Other informational means were weekly PTA newsletters, a PTA presentation, a parent workshop that offered some of the same activities their children experienced, an Art Walk (a guided discussion as parents viewed the all-school exhibition in the hallways), and a training session for parents who accompanied the third and fourth graders on trips to the art museum.

A kindergarten teacher, two first-grade teachers, a fourth-grade teacher, and I established a monthly teacher-as-researcher group that enabled us to collaborate on our questions about classroom research and inquiry. From this I discovered more about the students, ways to connect to the school curriculum, and the connections the students were making from their work in the art room to other subjects. For example, I learned that Gina, a fourth grader, approached her writing through her art. I found that the kindergarten students were showing new abilities in talking about art, telling what they saw in a painting or what story they were reminded of. I also learned that first graders were planning their art projects before they arrived in the art room.

Learning more about the community and involving the community by providing information about our process resulted in informal, ongoing conversations throughout the year that gave me added knowledge about the impact of art at the school. A veteran kindergarten teacher described how comfortable her students were about discussing art, an opportunity she never had as a child. Parents willingly recounted their children's conversations about art at home; one told me, "Last night my daughter began talking about her favorite artist!" I made the transition from teaching eighth-grade English to elementary art, from daily to weekly meetings with my students. In order to create a workshop that went beyond just making pictures to connecting the work to the children's emerging literacy, it was important to show the process of learning, to inform through exhibition and presentation, and to encourage and continue to seek out collaboration with teachers and parents.

If the arts and other special subjects are to become central to learning, teachers need to move beyond their own classrooms and observe their students in other contexts. Reaching out to parents and teachers, encouraging them to see the artists workshop as a laboratory of emerging literacy, opened up possibilities for all of us. Teachers began to understand that children learn in many modes, through many facets of their intelligence, and that they can be encouraged to continue to draw a connecting line between reading, writing, and the arts. This collaboration in learning extended to my students, who saw me engaged in drawing and writing as they moved through the doors of the art room.

Drawing and Writing: Partners in Classroom Research

"You're a real artist, aren't you?"

"That's what real artists do."

These were typical comments I heard as my students passed me on their way to recess. I often sat outside in the yard next to the open door of my classroom, drawing and writing in my journal. When parents stopped by the school, they commented about how important it was for the students to see this kind of modeling. My role as a practicing artist-writer, using drawing as a meaning-making tool, was essential to my understanding as a researcher and my relationships with students, parents, and faculty. I collected data mainly through observations in my spiral sketch journal, where I used drawings as a way to record the experiences of the day, reflect on what they meant, consider how I could take action on what I was learning, and connect me to my past classrooms. Constant writing put me in touch with my former eighth-grade community and the elements that framed it. Writing also put me in touch with my own experiences in art as a child, giving me a goal in this classroom to provide an environment that encouraged a sense of accomplishment in children. Writing can help teachers be conscious of the experiences, events, and passions they bring to a new classroom situation; drawing was my way to begin observing the unfamiliar, in other teachers' classrooms or in my own. Drawing Allen and Martin as they wrote in their artists notebooks (see overleaf) focused my concentration, enabling me to be present for their work in the classroom, to record both the experience and the context. Words and pictures worked in partnership as tools to describe meaning. Drawing Robbie while he painted (see page 33) led me to a question I asked my students: "Think of yourself as a painter. What do you feel, see, discover as you paint?" Drawings were the catalyst for my thinking and writing. It was as I drew Kim and Christy, two first graders at work at their table, that my writing helped me think about expanding the artists notebooks to the younger grades. My writing and drawing worked as partners as I drew Brenda, robed in her green striped smock, working at her table on her painting. I focused on her painting, and that led me to interview her; her words filled the spaces around the drawing (see page 34). For me, recording the words with the drawing captured the moment.

Noticing, then drawing, made me question closely, prompted me to move inside my students' thinking, inside their work. Drawing Carl as he leaned over his work showed me that he was working on writing, not on a picture. As I captured Brendan in his smock, I also noticed

Kim and Christy painting their underlying masks

Carl leans down over his notebook where it spreads over the floor.
"What are you doing — drawing or something?"
"Did I make you mess up?"

Allen keeps his collage right next to him while he does a drawing of it in his notebook.

— Martin diligently & his body close in, tongue pressing down as he goes in close. backs up. from his notebook

What's going on in you
What's going on in room.
What have you learned?

It is a blue sky and a perfect fall day —
not too hot — breezy — and I feel
zoomed up — so much so that I haven't
been able to do much — so I am writing
to think. (Actually I am enormously
inspired today and can't think straight).
I suffer from over stimulation.

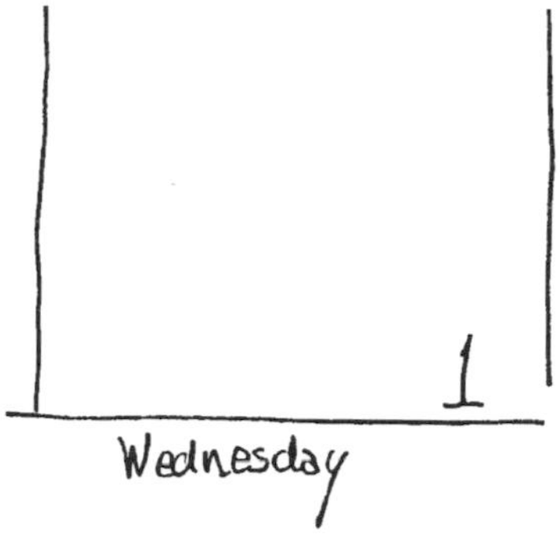

1

Wednesday

Think of yourself
as a painter —
think of our painting
We have painted like
Kandensky & Jackson —
We have painted
with feelings.
We have made a mask
What colors have
you made?
What has gone on
in your mind.
What have you
seen in this room
Let it run like a
video-tape. Write down
those images.

an interview w/ Brenda

Deana gave me
an idea when she
said she was going
to do the woods so I
made grass & flower
and then when I saw
Deanie make pink
I thought of making
pink roses.

"The rose woods"

It's kind of happy and
sad because of greens —
well one of the trees is
a bright green

I added
light blue
Do you like it
yes —
because of the
roses & sky.

what did you
discover? —
By accident
I put some
brown right
here so I
thought a tree
could go here.

his new attempt at painting, leading me to question him further. One day, as most of the fourth-grade students were working on masks, I noticed that two boys had not attempted a mask and were spending a long time making a decision about their media. As I moved over, encouraging them to try, they explained they were not very good mask makers. This startled me: just ten years old and already dismissing a possibility for new learning! I wondered about achieving balance between providing choice and giving direction, about shifting the locus of control. Writing, reflecting, and questioning provided the impetus to take action on these areas of tension. Other questions and considerations tumbled in my mind: about the use of portfolios, about writing, about my role as teacher, about evaluation, about my art, about the importance of exhibition, about the need to take risks with my youngest students. The writing took me back to my former experiences, helped me find answers for teaching, relieved my own tension in this new situation, and helped me continue to risk, to move into the unknown. I wrote in my journal that January:

> This is the hardest part because I have a tendency to feel unsure about letting them go; I think if I show them how and they do as I do they'll do better. But my experience of twenty-one years tells me differently: if I model, talk, show, do, write, and ask—they will go beyond anything I have imagined: like Brenda's peach color yesterday, her delicate dots of poppies in the field, or Christina's collage of mixed-media faces. When I let go, my students begin informing me as an artist as former students informed me as a writer. That is an excitement in the classroom that is irreplaceable.

Drawing and writing were essential to my work as a researcher and to the way in which my students related to me; they helped me capture my students' images, understand their learning, and recall the knowledge I drew from experience. I was reminded of the power of sitting next to my former students as they worked, questioning their process and their intentions. As Ruth Hubbard (1991) puts it, "If we invite children to become our ethnographic informants, we can begin to understand their world on their terms, without falling prey to preexisting assumptions about their abilities. In this new role, the child is not the passive 'subject' of the research, but an active collaborator" (13).

A Collection of Words and Pictures

It's this moment that I love — when I meet one student artist as a colleague — he taught me today

Jamie stood at his space, tearing the form of a giraffe out of bright yellow paper. He reached for strips of black from the pile of colored construction paper he had spread across the table. He placed the torn pieces and strips next to the white sheet and, while still standing, he began to draw big, bold strokes of crayon. As he worked he began to piece together a puzzlelike giraffe, alternating with continued crayon strokes. His hand moved from a tan streaked background to the leaves in a palm tree while he adjusted the yellow paper of the giraffe. I sat down next to him as he concentrated intently on his work. I was drawn to this intriguing picture and wanted to ask him about it. He never looked up from his collage as I began.

"Where did you get your idea for this?" I asked.

"I saw a picture you showed us, a tiger. I wanted to draw then from that . . . a giraffe. [That book] got me to draw animals. When I drew that other thing of giraffes, then I wanted to do this." Jamie went on to say that "to get ideas from paintings, from other kids" had been a big help to him in the artists workshop.

My field notes in words and pictures, like those I made of Jamie, formed the core of data for my study; they filled twenty-two research journals. Additionally, the children's own work—Jamie's picture of the giraffe, Brenda's picture of a tree and a meadow, Bob's picture inspired by a fourth grader, and hundreds more pieces of artwork, along with the students' writing—were significant parts of my data. I "read" the pictures of my students as I looked through their portfolios and as I walked around the room to see how they were progressing in order to help me offer new choices for next time. A collection of their pictures provided the story for the school exhibitions and, in a similar way, contributed to the collage of stories that is this book.

Students' pictures, as in the case of Jamie's giraffe collage, led me to question further, not stopping at the pictures. The pictures invited me to step inside the thinking of the child and encouraged my new, younger students to become my "curricular informants" (Harste and Rowe). Informal interviews, notes of conversations about students' work, discussions of work during rehearsal, and talk about pictures displayed in the hallways gave me additional layers of information. Jamie's picture attracted my attention to his work; my picture recorded our interaction; our conversation led me to understand that his idea came from the literature we read and that collaborating with other students was essential to his work. Students' writing in their artists notebooks about their pictures provided more information—about their thinking, their process, their plans, their questions. Jamie's giraffe picture made him feel like a real artist. He wrote, "What stands out for me is when you said that girl gave you a picture and it made you feel like an artist. I remember when I drew my giraffe picture." Students indicated the positive effect of being recognized, took pride in their work, and expressed the importance of having their own projects. Supporting these words and images were audiotapes of teacher interviews, students' informal conversations while they worked, and our more formal discussions of art, literature, and their projects.

Recalling the work of other researchers who suggest that teacher-researchers can learn by closely observing and interviewing a few individual students who become "key informants" (Bogdan and Biklen, p. 63), I selected four students, Alice, Carl, Christina, and Jessica, to watch and interview. Over time I observed their intensity and interest in their work—when Carl added "van Gogh" to his name, for example, or when Christina came to the workshop during recess. I found that their openness to expressing themselves through words and pictures pushed me as an artist. The portraits of and conversations with these four students are offered in Chapter 4. My interviews with them were like conversations and, like the connecting quality of the line from my own drawing pen or Jamie's bold strokes of the crayon, they add to the emerging picture of this workshop.

Just as Jamie began his collage with a pile of colored construction paper and crayons, I began this book with my own pile of colored construction paper: twenty-two one-hundred-page research journals filled with drawings, observations, impressions of hundreds of students and their artworks; interviews; photographs and videotapes of the classroom; artists notebooks; schedules; and the letters I wrote to my students from the artists workshop. And just as Jamie worked with determination toward his impression of a jungle, selecting colors and pieces to get there, my process in analyzing this collection of material was driven by a sense of the whole. This helped me to join words and pictures—mine and my students'—and to tell the story of this experience. Before I could assemble my collage, I analyzed and selected my data and began to identify themes, which for me became the bold strokes of color that held together these pictures of learning.

A Collage of Stories

I have chosen to present my findings in a collage of stories where words and pictures work together. As I moved around my new classroom observing Jamie, Alice, Carl, Jessica, and the others, I knew that there was more going on than "just making pictures." Although art class was seen as marginal or "extra" and the art teacher was called "special," I nonetheless believed that the arts were a valuable way of making meaning. I knew from experience how drawing helped me create meaning as a researcher. I believed that the arts and the art program needed to be central to the emerging literacy of children. With that belief in mind—and in hand—I found I could only tell and show the story through images written and drawn.

3
Pieces of the Collage
ELEMENTS OF THE
EMERGING WORKSHOP

Two teachers from another middle school observed our writers workshop as our routine continued. I sat close to Andrea, one of the eighth graders, at the conference table, listening to her story, questioning her, and learning as she discussed her idea of having the voice change midway through her piece in progress. We seemed suspended on this island in the midst of the rest of the class as some students conferred in small groups, some huddled in a corner writing, and others talked about what they were planning to write. I noticed one student standing and staring out the window. Bursts of laughter rang out as I picked up a bit of the latest eighth-grade gossip. In our writers workshop I provided my students with a structure, a routine, freedom, and coaching while Andrea and my other students, involved in their own projects, showed me new possibilities about writing and learning.

The two visitors watched this process for several periods, then approached me and asked, "Is this what you do every day?" Interrupted by a new class entering the room and a student requesting a conference, I nodded, wondering if they understood the layers of learning here. Behind this seemingly simple picture was intense thinking, powerful ownership of learning, and expanded collaboration between teacher and students.

Although to some the eighth-grade writers workshop appeared simple, to others, who took the time to analyze, the complexities were apparent. Similarly the picture of our artists workshop concealed a collage of elements, layers of learning, and emergent themes that formed the framework. The artists workshop was propelled by my vision of a workshop parallel to the writers workshop.

Artists Workshop, Writers Workshop

A third-grade class entered the art room, followed the directions on the easel, and sat on the rug by the red-house banner in the sharing area. Our workshop began with a rehearsal for learning (see Graves). On this day I displayed a work by Kandinsky, thinking it might prompt the students to visit a small exhibit of Kandinsky's original work at a local gallery. In our daily rehearsal we looked at art to understand what real artists do, we studied illustrations to see how words and pictures worked together, and we listened to stories to help inspire and encourage us to open our imagination. In the rehearsal in writers workshop the students and I sat in a circle, wrote together, shared our writing, read works of other authors, and learned to listen to each other. In both workshops, sharing work by students or professional artists built a community of learners, helped students learn to discuss art and literature, and provided them with ideas for their own work.

I took status of the class, asking that they tell me what media they would use or the topic for their pictures. I watched with anticipation as everyone got their materials and went to work. Self-selecting topics for writing and books for reading in the writers workshop led me to encourage students in my art class to select their own topics for picturing, drawing, painting, and pasting. Taking status of the class helped me focus on student choice.

Writing itself became one of the art forms, as some students spent their hour in art working on a poem or a story. As one student painted, I sat down and brainstormed with him a list of words inspired by his picture. Emma worked on a collage series, prompted by poems she had written in her classroom upstairs (see Figure 3–1).

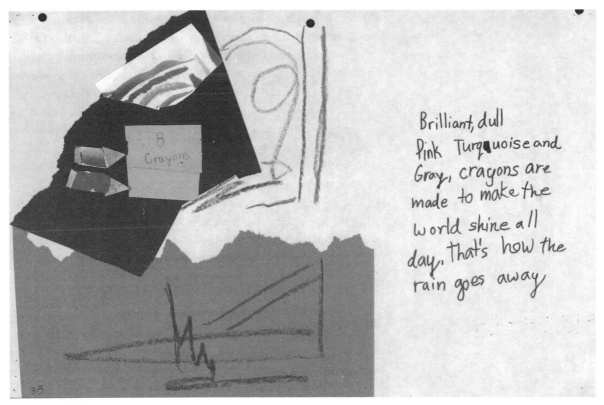

Brilliant, dull
Pink Turquoise and
Gray, crayons are
made to make the
world shine all
day, that's how the
rain goes away

FIGURE 3–1
One of Emma's series of collages/poems.

Note taking in my research journal and record keeping through taking status of the class began to help me know what we would do next, and as students made choices in painting, collage, writing, and mixed media, they showed me possibilities beyond what I proposed. I sat next to my students while they worked, feeling less the need to watch over or direct them than moved to question what they were making and what inspired them, constantly noting the stories that were embedded in the pictures they created.

Evaluation and assessment were ongoing, propelled by student choice and my role as an observer. As in my writers workshop, I did not grade individual pieces of writing or pictures or keep a grade book with quiz scores and numbers. Instead, I kept a chart with a narrative on each student's progress, evidence of our conferences, my questioning and observations, our shared learning, and their published writing and pieces in progress. Whole-class response to work led to personal reflection and ongoing evaluation and stimulated students to engage in their own projects, not those assigned by me.

In both workshops students kept all of their work in portfolios, including mistakes and plans for stories and pictures. I discouraged them from throwing away work. I emphasized that artists learn from their mistakes and later often use sketches, ideas, or starts found in their portfolios. As Cal brought a collage of a car to show me, I suggested he try adding big splotches of torn paper. Later his smile told me what he thought of his revised creation, and he asked me to help him frame it for the next exhibition.

The opening exhibition of children's work, on display in the hallways, stimulated further work in the artists workshop. Students would immediately begin selecting possible pictures for the next exhibition, mounting those works on colored construction paper at our Frame Shop, a corner of the studio with stacks of colored construction paper, a paper cutter, staplers, and glue. As students selected work from their portfolios for the publishing board in the writers workshop or the hallway exhibitions in the artists workshop, they were involved in self-assessment. A consciousness to go public propelled their ongoing work. The valuable learning I gained from the end-of-quarter conference in the writers workshop led me to create a portfolio review in the artists workshop (see Chapter 5).

Collaboration in both workshops was important in developing a classroom of good art and writing teachers. Just as students met in peer groups to confer over writing and get response to works in progress, here students sat at tables together discussing their work and sharing their processes of picture making. In writers workshop students shared unfinished pieces within the classroom in group share or from the Author's Chair and published their writing for a wider audience on the eighth-grade publishing board in the hallway outside the classroom. Similarly, in the artists workshop, pictures were shared during our rehearsal on the rug, and the work informed a wider audience of parents, teachers, and other students when students displayed pictures and words in the all-school exhibitions in the hallways. Publishing and exhibition extended collaboration and learning.

Writing about the process of thinking and learning was essential in both workshops. In writers workshop students wrote about their writing process, used writing to rehearse for further writing, wrote letters to each other about independent reading, and developed essays that evolved from personal dialogue with literature. In artists workshop students recorded their thinking in their artists notebooks. They wrote about their picture making and their process, used writing to express meanings in their pictures, and wrote letters about the pictures exhibited in the hallways. Writing in both workshops helped the community develop through reading written thoughts aloud.

In writing and reading with my eighth-grade students I not only modeled for them but learned with them how to be a better reader and writer. In the artists workshop, I continued to be part of a community of learners. When my young students wrote I wrote with them, sharing my thoughts, my new learning. As the workshop moved closer to my vision of it, their work as inquiring artists inspired me to engage in my own inquiry as an artist, pushing the margins of my own creativity as I worked with the same materials as my students.

As I worked and learned with my eighth-grade students, there were times when I pulled back. I made myself an observer of the workshop in process, raising questions with my students, collecting their work to help me understand their learning, and changing the workshop based on what I found out. Observation also played a key role in the emerging artists workshop, in my learning about my new, younger students and about the role of the arts in literacy. This new workshop of learning came about as a result of my experiences in my former classrooms. It confirmed my belief that teachers are like artists. All teachers need a vision and the skill as an observer to let their learning with their students help form new pictures of classroom communities and workshops of learning. With a vision based on experience and on the work of others in education, teachers can be like artists, not worrying about the absolute lesson or following a linear curriculum, but desiring to make each class an approximation of the picture they imagine. My process as a reflective practitioner helped me constantly revise and refine the workshop toward my vision and include new learning from my students as well as their projects, goals, and needs.

Nancie Atwell (1990) describes a workshop of learning as one "in which writing and reading are learned in the richest possible context and appreciated as tools of the highest quality for helping children come to know about the world" (p. xxii). As I learned more about teaching younger children and a new discipline, I wanted the work in the art room to become a learning workshop. Here the arts provided the richest possible context, as I intended our work in the artists workshop to bring the arts into literacy, believing that the arts are essential ways of knowing the world. In examining the complementary processes of drawing and writing in a first-grade classroom, Ruth Hubbard (1989) writes, "Pictures as well as words are important to human beings in their communication; we need to expand our narrow definition of literacy to include visual dimensions, and in so doing answer the call of researchers for the recognition of multi-literacies *and* ways these literacies can work to complement each other" (p. 150). In this workshop we would not limit ourselves to what pictures looked like; instead, we would explore the thinking that went into their making and use writing as a powerful tool to help us make sense of the experiences. I formed this new workshop for the convenience of my young artists and writers, ready for the unpredictable and complex nature of creating.

In presenting a picture of the artists workshop in this chapter, I describe each element that formed the framework. These elements parallel those in a writers workshop and are based on the following concepts:

> Writing and picturing are complementary processes.
> Literature can be used in and beyond rehearsal.
> There is an innate tension between student choice and teacher direction.
> Collaboration is essential; students and teacher must engage in learning together.
> Exhibition of student work can extend learning.
> Apprenticeships can encourage and enhance learning.

The room was silent as the students glanced at a picture they had selected from their portfolios, then wrote in their artists notebooks. I had asked this class of fourth graders to write down what they saw in their picture, what they felt as they looked at it, what title they would give the piece.

After several minutes of silent writing, hands went up as students wanted to share. Renee read from her artists

To Write a Piece of Art: Writing and Picturing as Complementary Processes

notebook the words describing a torn-paper collage in her portfolio:

"Title: black hole"; "spacey," "colorful," "confetti," "unpieced crayon," "gold rush?" "mountains," "unmade shapes." Her written thoughts led to a work where words and pictures worked together to express meaning (see Plate 10).

Black Hole

See and create
Watch and create
Work toward an ending
   Of confetti
To describe it.
Watch a gold rush
   or unpiece a crayon.
Each is a work of art
Bit of space
   scraps of paper
Make up shapes
   use unmade ones
Try a masterpiece
   You're an artist.

After doing a careful line drawing of a pot of geraniums (see Plate 1), Allen wrote, "It is easier to write about something you see with your eyes." Pictures led to words. As in Renee's and Allen's work, the linking of the visual with the written gave students ways to express their uniqueness and their creative thought, thereby widening their abilities to say what they meant. Writing gave Renee freedom to use language to describe what she saw. Allen's words began to describe the ways pictures helped him make meaning.

Artists Notebooks: Answers, Inquiries, Meanings
All third and fourth graders kept artists notebooks, following the example of artists, writers, and scientists, who use writing and art as part of their work in their studios and

laboratories, recording in them their discoveries and thought processes. My students used their notebooks to develop ideas, sketch plans, and think about their pictures' meanings. In her study of the processes of experienced thinkers, Vera John-Steiner found that "it is by means of language that poets, writers, and philosophers, who are driven by the need to think beyond the limits of the known, have attempted to share with others their personal inquiries" (p. 111). In my workshop it was through writing that students explored and shared with me their personal inquiries.

As students balanced on their stools in the classroom studio, their gray folders opened in front of them, they initially wrote in response to questions I posed: What did you discover? What is your picture about? What do you plan to make? One boy wrote, "I learned the more I was making the picture the more it became different." "An alligator pattern," was another student's response. Someone else wrote, "I need to finish cutting my picture." Others, like Matt, expressed a sense of real accomplishment. "Today the teacher framed my picture with orange paper. The teacher also said I need a poem for my spatter painting. . . . " Writing revealed the thinking, planning, and discovering that occurred in their picture making.

Through writing I began to understand what was inside the spattered picture, the pages of scribble, the bold strokes of color. Writing helped me see that there was more going on than making pictures. Robbie wrote in his artists notebook, "Today i had a grat ecsperience. I finished my mask and got to do a painting, mixed new colors and art has been good to me." As Emma leaned over next to me right before her classmates shared their writing, she whispered, "I wrote a whole page." Through continuous sharing of student work, her classmates and I learned the secrets and surprises within the ongoing work. Writing together helped us work as authentic learners, using writing to help think about what pictures meant. "I think my picture looks like a river with a bridge and a sunset behind a mountain." Others wrote about their process. "I just ripped paper, making more things with ripping the paper." I learned what inspired them, from the books they were reading to their thoughts and personal experiences. One student described his picture made with crayons as "a place in Norway where I have a cabin next to a lake with mountains behind the lake." Students described what they learned: "When you're making a collage and you overlap you can make neat and weird shapes." Students described what they accomplished: "This is the third time I've been to art this year and I've already done two projects. The first one is called 'Abstract' the second one is called 'Louisiana.'"

Kindergartners through second graders told of their discoveries as I recorded their thoughts in a large sketch pad, their community artists notebook. They announced that "colors change to other colors" or "Jessica and I have been asking each other what we want to make." This record of their words showed that their work, just as that of the older students, included invention, surprise, collaboration, and more. The combination of writing and pictures evident in the classroom led them to begin asking me to write their stories on their pictures as they worked.

My intention in making writing an essential element in the workshop was not only to allow students to draw as they learned how to write but to encourage both visual and verbal expression. Writing helped students think about what they were making and what they planned to make, thus prompting them to come to the workshop ready to choose their own projects. For some students writing in the artists notebook became a necessary form of note taking, helping them remember where they were as projects continued from one week to the next. One boy asked, "Can I write [my collage] down so I don't forget where I am?" My students' writing allowed me to learn the ways they used writing and revealed their ongoing inquiries and arrivals at meaning.

I began to see that students could, should, come to the workshop with their own projects and ideas. My role was to provide them with literature, art, and technique as they moved forward. With the possibility of writing always there and encouraged, students began to use it as a tool in their class work, thus revealing more about their thinking and creating. Writing sharpened students' ability to look at and consider what they saw in their own pictures. In her first entry a fourth grader wrote, "I would call my first picture 'Blue Mountain and Golden River.' I just kept tearing out pieces and never thought about it until I was finished and I really looked at it. I could see a blue mountain and a golden river. It really didn't change, like I said I really didn't think about it." Without writing, meanings would have been private; students would have focused on the appearance of pictures or on my interpretations. Another student was able to describe in writing how looking was an important act in making pictures: "It helped me see that even though you might make something that you don't like, you can change it and make it something you do like."

Writing as a Form of Assessment

My students' writing helped me assess their work, helped me know that they were beginning to experience the art room as an artists workshop, that my focus on thinking, writing, the environment, and our community experience was having an effect. One student wrote, "When I paint I feel like I am in a studio." The writing held a range of ideas, from the introspective words of Ellen ("What I see does not matter. What I know does not matter. It only matters what I see and know together") to the straightforward answers of students like Jill ("I got my idea from an art book. My picture doesn't look like anything, I didn't learn anything, [I discovered] nothing"). Many students reminded me that there was more than art on their mind as they came to the art room, helping me remember their wide world of learning and discovery.

The act of writing and the emphasis on thinking—not on the way pictures looked—helped students acquire the tools of close observation, use their imagination, describe their own process, and assess their own work. As Thomas described it, "I really like art writing. I like thinking and writing about my art." He often made what he called designs. Writing helped him assess what he was doing. Even though he was dissatisfied with his pictures, he was able to describe how he wanted to change as an artist: "Today I drew three pictures. Two were very weird, one looked like a sleigh with wheels, the other was a shack. My last one I hate. It's all sloppy and boring. . . . I think I made too many designs and should start making more real things, like a forest or a town or a city. Next time I might do something like that." Emma concluded, "If I could be more interested in imagination, I think I could be a better artist." Sandy described how she was learning to look and think about her work in a new way. "Now I study it and put myself in it and I think how I like it in my picture."

Writing helped students revise their pictures. Ellen's painting of trees and a pond (see Plate 2) had inspired many students in other classes to try their own versions. She found it difficult to describe in writing her process of making the picture. But after having struggled to write about, then sketched, her painting in her notebook (see Figure 3–2), Ellen said she had forgotten something. Unpinning her painting from the board, she returned to the work table and added the reflection of the trees in the pond. Writing and sketching in her notebook helped her revise her picture, linking the complementary processes in an important way.

Emma chose to combine watercolor and crayons (see Figure 3–3), describing her process in writing: "I used the feelings that I saw in my work. I thought it would only take ten or fifteen minutes, but it took my imagination instead."

Writing in our artists workshop—as in any subject, in any workshop of learning—intensified thinking, led to the

Today I painted a
picture of the woods.

It looks

like this.

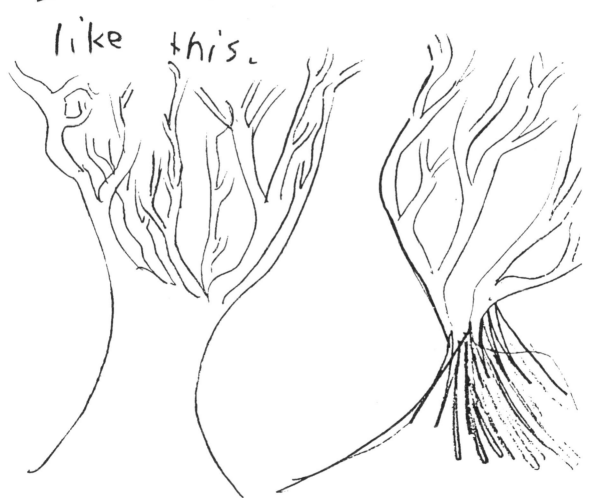

FIGURE 3–2
A page from Ellen's notebook.

FIGURE 3–3
Emma's watercolor-and-crayon landscape.

formation of new ideas, and aided understanding. Writing in the artists workshop helped students see, think, say, sort out, understand, and imagine. Students began using writing and picture making separately and together to express themselves. Jake wrote, "I've become a better writer and that writing goes to my pictures. I think I've become better at drawing and painting. I've learned how to mix more colors. I've learned how to look at pictures more closely and the feeling of that picture." Writing and picturing were forms of meaning making, and with writing as a key element in the workshop, pictures and words worked together as complementary processes of knowing and provided a link between words and images.

Writing as Art, Art as Writing

At times students described art as writing and writing as art. Emma wrote, "My whole writing time was spent looking at different poses of a horse," while Lawrence wrote in his notebook, "In art you don't just write a piece of art and then say you're done. First you imagine what you're going to make, then imagine where you are going to put the colors. Then when you're finished drawing, you see how much better your painting is when you imagine." In the artists workshop, students were writing pieces of art and turning writing into art.

As questions surfaced about the emerging workshop, about the connections between writing and images, the students' writing taught me how painting and making pictures were true forms of expression. "I can express myself with paintings. Paintings are the only way to be truthful about how you feel inside and what you're really like," wrote Martin. Painting led to feelings of self-confidence: "I feel good as a painter it makes all my feelings shine through. I think painting is just another form of words ... when I paint I feel good all over. When I am painting I feel important. I may not be very good at it but I still like it anyways."

ʌA Momentary Rush Of Water on the Rio Grande ʌ

ʌ I feel a smooth cool draft of air.
opace, open space. All I see...A dam.
    Then suddenly, water rushing violently, on and on
never stopping. But only for a moment. ʌ

Rocket-smoke

Mechanical parts, and metal bars,
all on a sunny day,
I walk through an empty field,
exept for a rocket.
Suddenly I'm in a planitarium.
I turn my picture upside down,
A vase.with a face on top.
A beard, eyes, a nose, cheeks and a
mouth. Turn it back the right way
a falling building next to the
rocket.

Pictures led to words and the words revealed meanings, adding to the power behind the pictures. For example, Anthony wrote about making two of his pieces: "When I was painting, I felt happy. The colors streamed from my mind and each color had a meaning to be in the picture. Then when I was drawing I felt like I was climbing the mountains and my cabin was down below. The fresh air was in my lungs. It made me feel happy." Just as pictures led to words, words led to pictures. "Writing!" Martin called out as I took status of the class to record what my students planned to work on. Writing became one of the art forms, and some students spent their hour in art working on a poem or a story. Allen and Martin, who even asked to come in during their recess, worked on their poems (see margin), then created pictures. Just as Emma had brought her poems from her writers workshop to inspire her collages, a third grader's choice of a project in the artists workshop was influenced by his new learning in his regular classroom about metaphor and simile (see Figure 3–4). Two fourth-grade girls asked if they could "write poems" before they "did art."

Jonathan turned his feelings into words and his words into art: "It felt wild, wacky. It felt like a splash or colors. It felt strange, cold, warm. It felt different. Scary. It felt great. It felt like magic!" (see Figure 3–5). Jonathan and others found that pictures and the act of making them led to poetic, expressive writing. Through my students I discovered new meaning in the words of the American artist Walter Meigs: "Experience, even for a painter, is not exclusively visual." When words and pictures are made available and valued as ways of expression, learning can be experienced in bold strokes of words and in crafted lines of color.

Endings of Confetti

"I think that shapes and color show more than words. I can see world beyond world. I see bats, and caves, triangles, lines, repeats and unrepeats," wrote Dennis. Making and

Figure 3–4
A painting and poem inspired by metaphor.

It felt wild

wacky
It felt like a splash
or colors.
It felt strange,
cold, warm.
It felt different.
Scary.
It felt great.
It felt like magic!

FIGURE 3–5
A page from Jonathan's notebook.

looking at pictures were simultaneous processes, and for students like Dennis and Martin, paintings and pictures were the best way to express themselves, though words helped them express ideas and helped me understand the value of the visual as a way of knowing. Sandra found that art inspired her writing. She wrote, "Art is very important. It gives me ideas for what to write about. . . . It makes my imagination grow. . . . It lets me find and express my feelings." In the artists workshop writing and making pictures were partners, forms of discovery, ways of thinking, means of expression; and both were art forms. Art led to writing, writing led to pictures, and both were valued and used together in helping students use their imagination. Students were spilling words onto the page, following Renee's urging to "unpiece a crayon" and "work toward an ending of confetti."

Literature: In and Beyond Rehearsal

Literature, as part of the artists workshop, gave students ideas for pictures and projects and helped them decide on topics. Through reading literature, mainly picture books, students learned how pictures and written language work together.

"The book gave me so many ideas," a fourth grader remarked as he set to work after listening to S. W. Samton's *The World from My Window*. Kevin, a kindergartner, told me his picture was "the sun setting like the boy made in *The Legend of the Indian Paintbrush*" by Tomie dePaola and asked me to write this on his painting. Terry used writing to discover meaning in her own picture, finding she, too, was influenced by the literature read during the rehearsal segment of the class. She wrote, "Today I made a picture or collage that looked somewhat like the picture in the counting book that had collage pictures. Actually now that I think about it it looked exactly like it, and I didn't do it on purpose at all." Rather than use them prescriptively as story starters or models I intended to let works of poets, illustrators, and writers awaken something in students.

"It wasn't enough for Jackson that he could draw something perfectly and paint it exactly the color it seemed. 'It isn't enough anymore. . . . I want to capture the feeling.'" Students sat on the rug, their eyes never wavering from the delicate watercolor paintings of the pages of *Jackson Makes His Move* by Andrew Glass, reading the pictures as I read the words of the text. Jackson, a discouraged raccoon artist, was trying to make sense of his own work in art.

Alice, a very serious artist in first grade, was inspired by Jackson to experiment in media and worked for an entire hour on an abstract piece using markers and overlapping colors of wax sticks. *Jackson Makes His Move* helped students experiment in pictures and thinking, as swirls of line and color interpreted happy and sad feelings. Influenced by Jackson, one student asked, "Can I mix twelve feelings together in a painting?" *Jackson Makes His Move* helped me emphasize the idea that pictures don't always have to "be something," but that we need to try to think about what we are making, to consider what feeling we are trying to convey. I used literature to help my students become concerned with their thinking, build a vocabulary of language and skills in art, use their imagination, avoid realistic depiction, not worry about what pictures looked like. The work of Eric Carle and Leo Lionni led students to paint papers, and to tear and cut them, incorporating them into collage (see Plate 7). Similarly, literature helped me shape the direction of the workshop by focusing a minilesson on the techniques used by illustrators: watercolor in *Jackson Makes His Move*, torn-paper collage in *Mouse Paint*, and cut-paper collage in *The World from My Window*. Cynthia Rylant's *All I See* and Tomie dePaola's *The Art Lesson* showed us the quest of an artist, and *Will's Mammoth* by Rafe Martin presented the possibilities of imagination (see Figure 3–6). Literature widened the range of possibilities for students' choices.

FIGURE 3–6
A student's imagined monster.

Literature is essential to any workshop of learning. It inspires, it opens doors to the imagination, to possibilities. Children read for their own purposes and make connections between the books and their pictures. The artists workshop surrounded the children with literature and echoed what Ruth Hubbard (1989) found: that classrooms filled with literature, master writers, illustrators, and art "encourage total communication in students' literate behaviors" (p. 155).

Literature helped move the workshop toward choice and ownership. Students showed me the ways in which literature influenced their work. Their writing showed that ideas for pictures came from both literature read in the workshop and books read in their regular classrooms. Again, this connected to their whole learning by providing a way for them to reflect on their personal inquiry in literature. Allen wrote, "My drawing was of a lake with ducks, geese, fish, turtles, a squirrel, a log, trees, and rock. The book *The Trumpet of the Swan* [by E. B. White] inspired me to draw this picture. In [it] there was a lake just like mine. The log was supposed to be the log Sam sat on. Also the lake behind my house inspired me."

Once my students became empowered to do their own projects, tension arose between letting them go and continuing to read stories, to discuss and look at art in our rehearsal, to demonstrate technique in minilessons. I knew that when art and literature are both made part of the process and rehearsal of learning, students' options are greater, their imagination opens, and their projects are of higher quality.

Tension: Student Choice, Teacher Direction

"Are we gonna do art today, or are you going to read us a story?" Bonnie asked as she preceded the rest of her second-grade class into the room, moving back toward the rug in the sharing area.

I looked up from my journal, thought for a moment, and answered, "Both."

On another day, Jessica asked, "Can we paint today?" just as the fourth-grade class she was in settled at the tables in the work area, ready to begin writing before I took status of the class. Although I had planned to offer a choice of media—markers, crayons, pencils—I had intended my students to continue with their drawing. I stared across the classroom, not having an immediate response, aware of being caught between wanting to give the students choices and needing to stay in control. Jessica interrupted my thinking as she added, "I wanted to paint my feelings today."

"We'll write to start, then I'll know," I responded.

Jessica's teacher had mentioned that Jessica already knew what she was going to do in art this week. Even though curiosity about Jessica hovered in my mind, I proceeded without asking her intentions. As we wrote I considered that part of my vision was to make this a workshop where students came with their own ideas for work. The tension between that notion and a teacher's need to feel in control had made me hesitate as I answered Bonnie and Jessica. This tension, sure to exist in a workshop when students begin finding their own voice and their own projects and media, is an element that needs to be anticipated and understood.

Teachers are frequently faced with this tension; they are reluctant to infringe on the freedom of students as they create. A workshop of learning is not, as some have described it, unstructured; it does not give totally free choice to students. A workshop of learning, in this case an artists workshop, must provide a balance between modeling the work and a chance for students to apply that knowledge to their own ideas for projects. There must be time for all: reading, showing, sharing, and working on individual projects.

I knew that students interpreted the work of others and developed their ideas for projects from their own perspective. I remembered Tom's moving piece on knowing his father for the first time, inspired by a novel he had read

in our eighth-grade writers workshop. I remembered Jen's choosing to use only poetry and watercolors to express her new learning in her report on aesthetic education. I knew from experience that when the work of artists and writers is used as a focus, students are empowered to find unique ways of understanding and expressing themselves, and use these models in ways far beyond my expectations.

In the artists workshop I watched third graders begin to understand perspective as they sat in the Gallery and copied a painting. I knew that reading *Mouse Paint* and other stories would help me begin the work of focusing on the visual and verbal in the artists workshop and that showing a painting by Monet would help me teach light, brushstroke, and the concepts of impressionism. The workshop must offer authentic activities in reading, writing, and creating and an atmosphere that values the work of writers, artists, and children while encouraging choice and ownership. The tension lies in trying to balance the important elements for the benefit of the teacher and the students, participants in their respective inquiries of learning.

Part of the tension in the artists workshop also came from students who would not move beyond writing the same story or drawing the same picture. I watched with dismay as one boy continued to draw pictures portraying violence, always using a pencil and ruler. I wondered why he was not inspired by the literature and art provided. I felt off balance: I was allowing him to choose, but I was not satisfied with his choice. That sense of imbalance pushed me to inquire about tension as it related to each student and to each class.

Choice was essential to the artists workshop, just as it had been to my writers workshop. I learned from my students that they were coming to this workshop with their own plans, inspired by a wide range of influences, and with questions that constantly pushed my inquiry and teaching. It took Jessica, and others throughout the year, to remind me of this. In writing about teaching, Donald Murray stresses that students must be given four freedoms: the ability to find their own subject, their own evidence, their own audience, and their own form. For Jessica, freedom to find her own form included visual as well as verbal solutions, paint as well as crayons, markers, and pens. The status of the class informed me of students' intentions, and I revised my plans based on their ideas. My own listening, observing, and writing allowed me to stay open and to take risks; my experience and vision informed my responses as Bonnie, Jessica, and others challenged my thinking throughout the year.

"Would anyone like to share?" My voice broke the silence at the end of five minutes of writing. Hands went up. My eighth graders and I wrote together, then shared our writing in order to listen to the beginning drafts of thinking, to hear individual voices, to learn from and know each other. I would take my turn last. My words revealed who I was, my starts as a writer, my thinking and learning in this classroom.

Susan's strong voice pierced the eighth-grade classroom as she read her acknowledgments before reading her piece: "I would like to thank my writing group, to Wendy for helping me conference, for helping me tell my true feelings without being afraid." She went on to thank the class for sharing their writing throughout the year, saying, "They inspired me to write new pieces."

My eighth graders showed me time and again that a classroom needs to be a community, built on trust, where students and teacher participate and respond as an audience of peers.

Christina, a fourth grader, stood at the Big Table, her smock covered with splatters of paint, while the first graders were hard at work on their own projects, across the room in the studio area. Christina frequently came to the art room during her recess while I continued teaching other classes. She had difficulty in reading and writing— English was her second language—and she worked closely with a tutor for her academic subjects. When Christina entered the art room, put on her smock, and set up the paints

Collaboration: Students and Teacher Learning

The reasons why I think the arts are ways of knowing

and a variety of materials, she took control of her learning, and even moved beyond my expectations and ideas for projects. When she created "Funny Faces," a work combining torn paper, paint, and crayon (see Plate 5), she took risks by experimenting with media and letting one idea lead to another. Christina's constant mixing of media, her messy smock, led me to view her as a budding artist, the way I had always wanted to be as I was growing up. Through genuinely engaging in my own learning, working as an artist and writer, I was a model for my students. Equally important, students like Christina were models for me. The classroom became a place for learning "where teacher and student both began to apply new knowledge, and to take control" (Atwell 1987b, p. 56).

Through this learning and collaboration, first with my eighth graders and now with my younger students, I became a better reader, writer, and artist. Christina inspired me with the possibilities of mixing media, Ellen showed me how writing helped her revise her painting, and Carl taught me how his use of writing was a form of note taking for "paintings he saw in his mind." Because of Christina's and other students' quests in expressing their ideas through pictures and words, I began taking time to work with the media I was offering them. They helped me move beyond only drawing in my journal, to begin experimenting with white crayon and watercolor and to capture images of my students with paint. They inspired me as an artist. They inspired one another by discussing their work in rehearsal and sharing their ideas as they worked. Collaboration as authentic learners—as writers, readers, and artists—was a powerful dynamic in our artists workshop. Writers learn from writers, artists learn from artists; here, students and teacher were inspired by and learned from one another.

Just as group share in writers workshop became a vehicle for helping my eighth-grade students become good writing teachers, looking at and discussing students' pictures helped my younger students become good art teachers. In rehearsal they learned to respond, to talk about one another's work, to express what they noticed, to consider why their eyes stopped at a particular picture as they scanned works in silence.

One of Brenda's paintings, along with nine other pictures from a variety of grades made after looking at work of the impressionists, was pinned to the board in the sharing area and was the focus of her second-grade class's discussion during rehearsal one day. Claire said she liked the way Brenda had painted the brown, that "it made it look like an island," and she liked "the way the flowers were bunched together." She said, "I can feel the wind blowing in the trees."

Brenda, a quiet student who had difficulty with written work in her regular classroom, described how she had made a green color, made a mistake, changed the color to brown, and then made a tree. Brenda told how her work had been inspired by other students. "Deana gave me an idea when she said she was going to do the woods, so I made grass and flowers and then when I saw Dennis make pink and I thought of making pink roses." Brenda got response from her classroom community, collected ideas as she worked, became the expert for her classmates, and quietly modeled her process. As she worked, she demonstrated the importance of collaboration within the workshop, and she was an example of how generative learning is when the classroom becomes a community.

Ellen's and Emma's paintings (see Plate 2 and Figure 3–3), in the same grouping as Brenda's, influenced Nicholas, a first grader, who asked to stay in art longer than the scheduled time to finish his picture. Nina, a first grader, called me over and asked: "Do you think my picture is good enough to go in a museum?" then told me her picture was inspired by both Monet and Ellen. As students constantly examined pictures from a variety of grades, they got new ideas for their work, stretched their use of technique, and went beyond expectations for their grade level or age. Just as group share in writing workshop enables writers to hear a range of perspectives or speak to a wider audience, here in the artists workshop students were influenced by one another, regardless of age or grade.

"Eeuw!" exclaimed Brittany as she looked at the new green Sondra was mixing on her palette. Caitlyn asked a fellow kindergarten classmate, "How did you make silver?" Students collaborated on everything from mixing a color out of the palette of primary colors to coming up with an idea for a picture or figuring out how to fix a mistake. Alice soon became an expert in the workshop; her first-grade classmates began walking over to her table to get her opinion of their latest picture. Students sitting together at her table collaborated and supported each other in their endeavors. Marla was highly influenced by Alice and often sought her advice as she worked. I observed how Marla's pictures had changed through her collaboration with Alice. Alice became her friend and teacher. Melinda became a teacher for Emily, a new student who spoke Swedish, as she taught her how to use paint, mix colors, and dab the colors onto the paper while Emily copied every stroke. Because personal projects coupled with collaboration and response were encouraged, the workshop was constantly filled with many teachers of all ages, ready to give answers when the questions came, guiding and suggesting in a nonthreatening way. Brenda had been inspired by the work of the impressionists; at the same time, she and Ellen were inspiring first graders. Students were there to teach and learn, to collaborate and respond.

In a second-grade class, Deana approached me. "I think I've changed a lot in making things.... Ever since we went outside I started getting more ideas ... and I've made this," she said, as she held up a crayon picture of the school. She elaborated on the differences she found between working inside the classroom and going outside to work, where she found she "was good at tennis courts and people."

As I got up from her table to get more paint for a student waiting at the paint cart, Deana beckoned me back: "I have more to say!" She continued to explain how she had changed and ended by asking me if she could share her process and picture with the class. In a workshop or classroom where collaboration and response are valued, students become an audience for one another and for their work; and, as Donald Murray says about writing, "Once the student has found an audience he will catch fire" (p. 119). Deana had her audience and a need to share her process and work; she needed to go public. Emphasis on collaboration helped students become reflective in their work, interested in their process of learning, excited to share, and eager to go public with new discoveries.

Students became teachers, artists, and experts while their classmates became a valued audience. Murray contends that the important role of a writing teacher is to create "an environment in which the student finds an audience of his [or her] peers and in which the audience of his [or her] peers has been trained to respond constructively to a piece of writing in process" (p. 119). In the artists workshop the students were trained as they learned to look at the way Brenda painted the brown, or discovered from each other how to make silver, or listened as Deana reported a breakthrough in her learning as an artist by discovering her imagination on the tennis court. Here, as in any workshop of learning, it is important for teachers to be engaged in writing, picturing, or whatever the activities within the discipline. Students and teacher must collaborate with one another. Then classrooms can be workshops where artists and writers, teacher and students, investigate their own sensibilities, their own margins, and provide opportunities to learn from one another in a setting where pictures, words, and solutions of many kinds are encouraged and valued. Here, where the environment encourages collaboration and response, teachers can help children become good art, writing, math, or science teachers.

Our all-school exhibitions extended the collaboration and provided a place for students to display their pictures and words and create a wider audience for their work. This inspired an exhibition consciousness, still another element of an atmosphere that propelled students "to catch fire."

Exhibition: Extending Learning

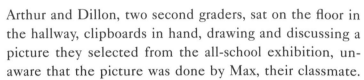

I watched my eighth graders and some younger middle-school students huddle around the eighth-grade publishing board in the hallway, reading Brad's latest published piece on the death of his friend. I thought how this kind of public sharing made Brad a much-talked-about author that day. Sharing, publishing, going public, was essential to the workshop; it stimulated and exhibited learning and widened the audience beyond just the teacher and classroom.

Arthur and Dillon, two second graders, sat on the floor in the hallway, clipboards in hand, drawing and discussing a picture they selected from the all-school exhibition, unaware that the picture was done by Max, their classmate.

Arthur remarked, "This is the awesome part," as he pointed to the curve in the road.

"I'll tell you, whoever drew this is good."

"Max!"

"Oh my gosh."

Arthur, Dillon, and other students were viewing the second all-school exhibition, extending their learning from the artists workshop to the hallways of the school. Like publishing in our writers workshop, which helped students find an audience and encouraged an enthusiastic attitude toward better writing, exhibitions were important elements in the artists workshop. Along with their classmates, Arthur and Dillon were engaged in an activity that focused on the work of students. They used drawing, conversation, and then writing to help them think, understand, see the works, and gain new ideas for their own work and new perspectives on their peers' work. Exhibitions allowed students to discover, collect new ideas, and share their

PLATE 1
Allen's geranium.

PLATE 2
Ellen's painting of trees and a pond.

PLATE 3
Matt's painting of a river.

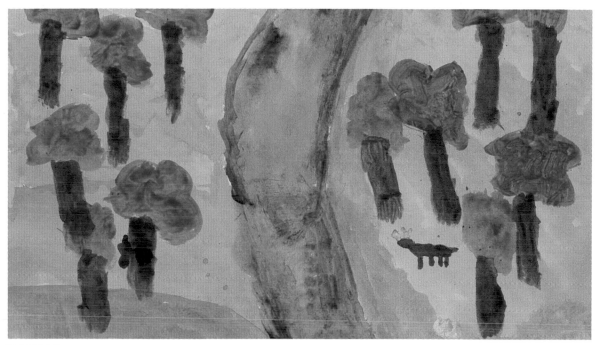

PLATE 4
"A River of Life."

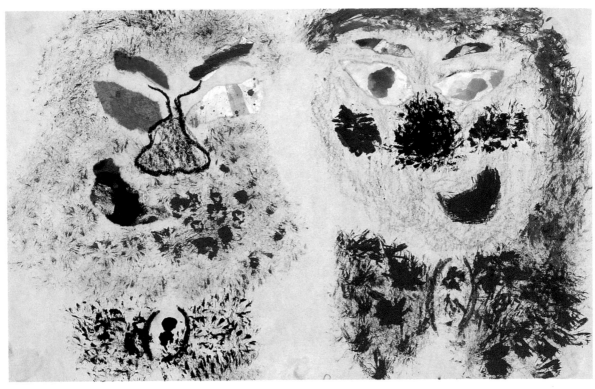

PLATE 5
"Funny Faces."

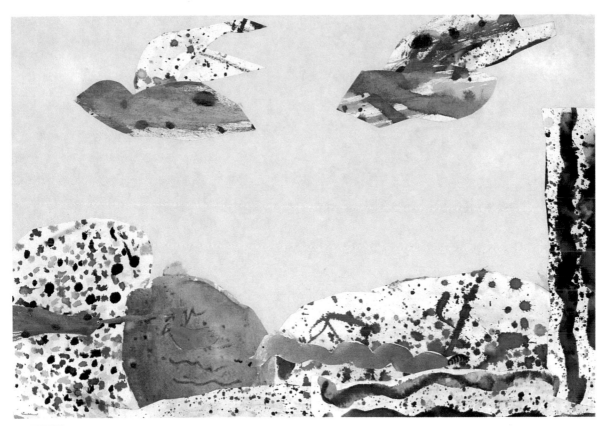

PLATE 6
Christina's collage.

PLATE 7
Collage inspired by literature.

PLATE 8
Dennis's poppy.

Picture of Wonders

To watch an artist
    splash paint
On his work of art.
To involve all his mind
    and feeling
Into his painting
To connect his
    work of art
With his movement of motions

PLATE 9
"Picture of Wonders."

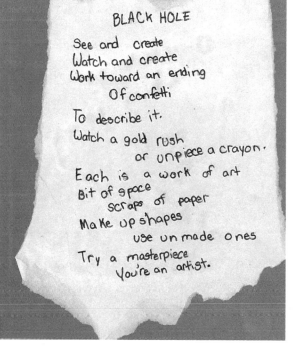

BLACK HOLE

See and create
Watch and create
Work toward an ending
    Of confetti

To describe it.

Watch a gold rush
        or unpiece a crayon.
Each is a work of art
Bit of space
    scraps of paper
Make up shapes
        use unmade ones
Try a masterpiece
    You're an artist.

PLATE 10
Renee's collage ("Black Hole").

PLATE 11
Alice's animal picture.

PLATE 12
"Beyond the Horizon."

thinking with their own classmates as well as students in other grades and classes. Four times throughout the year the school became a gallery, where some work of each child was exhibited. This provided an opportunity to inform teachers, parents, and students about the process of learning in the artists workshop and the ways children were using pictures and words together. A large poster announced the exhibition, and another poster, the exhibition catalog, described the work in the artists workshop over the months. Text panels were posted throughout the exhibition and explained the students' processes and their techniques, as well as their inspiration by other artists and writers.

As students, standing or sitting in the hallways, looked at the exhibit, their conversations were hushed, their attending serious, quiet, and focused. They noticed details ("I like this because it is lifelike"). They were able to discuss what they noticed ("I like this one because from far away they look like real flowers"). They took their looking seriously, discussing differences critically but not negatively. One older student remarked, "The first graders have more lines and curves, more ways of how they think into pictures." Many identified with the artist ("It reminded me of the vase of flowers we had at my grandma's"). Students showed pride in seeing their own work, and that of others, displayed. A classmate asked Allen, "Do you know the thing from your artists notebook is up there?"

When we were preparing for an upcoming exhibition, a hush prevailed throughout the workshop as students looked through their portfolios and selected a piece to display. They would continually ask me to frame their work as a possible piece for the next exhibition. Many students wanted to make a new picture or would ask, "When is the next poetry reading?" The poetry readings, so named by the students, were opportunities to show their pictures and read their accompanying writing in all-school music assemblies. Throughout the year, as students hung their work in the hallways, presented it in the music assemblies, and were encouraged to respond to pieces in the workshop, an exhibition consciousness developed. Through self-selecting pieces for these events, students learned to pore over their portfolios with a critical eye and consider their own work. It was an ongoing process of self-evaluation.

Following class visits to the all-school exhibitions, some students would write about the experience. Many described picking out a drawing they particularly liked, making quick sketches of a picture, discovering ideas. It made them feel like professional artists ("It felt like I was in a museum and it felt like being an artist"). Some described changed perceptions of a piece ("When I drew the pictures it made me feel weird because it looks like it has one color, black, but it doesn't"). Simon described the picture he looked at as being "a lot of things at the same time . . . a whale jumping in the water, or a creature, a tiger with many colors."

Other students chose to write to the artist whose work they had drawn and written about while in the hallway. Their letters would include a sketch, their interpretation of the original work. (The painting in Figure 3–7, for example, prompted the letter in Figure 3–8.) Grade boundaries were eliminated in this activity, as they were in many others: first graders would write to third graders, fourth graders to kindergartners. I found that letters were written most often for a social purpose, a way to communicate with someone in another grade. Kathleen, a third grader, showed she was interested in knowing Susan when she wrote: "Dear Susan, When I saw your picture it made me smile, and think of my little brother. You said you know me half a month ago on bus number one."

Letters also described what the writer was reminded of ("looks like a spaceship"). Sometimes a picture would remind two students of different things: "a bird flying over the ocean," "a whale jumping over the ocean." Other letters indicated that the pictures made students think of their families and, of course, pictures they had made them-

FIGURE 3–7
A student original from a hallway exhibit.

Dear Jason I like your picture. It reminds me of a caterpillar i found.

Sincerely,
Sidney

FIGURE 3–8
A fellow student's response to the above artwork.

selves. Many letters indicated surprise on the part of the viewer at the quality of work by someone "so young." One student questioned another, "Are you sure you are a first grader?"

Viewers had a wide range of reasons why they selected pictures, from simply "I lik your amagination" to shared areas of interest ("I like this because I'm interested in space, and I think that it's good to make art of it"). Some wrote that they simply thought the picture was "good." Letters described how looking at pictures evoked certain feelings: "Dear Kevin, Your picture gave me a lonely feeling, like an empty tent or a highway."

Writing encouraged and extended collaboration, while showing what inspired students and revealing what they noticed. Through their writing students were informing me about the layers of learning that occurred from drawing, painting, or viewing an exhibition. With writing as an essential part of this workshop of learning, I was able to go inside the thinking and learning of students as they experienced the exhibition.

Max's flag, Simon's painted trees, Jill's violin and flowers, were noticed, discussed, written about, copied, and reinterpreted by many students. These responses told me what students noticed, why they were drawn to a work, and what they thought was good. Students were using the learning they had gained through the work begun in the artists workshop. They were assuming responsibility for their learning and meaning making, and they were communicating their ideas with others. Exhibitions provide a means for teachers to learn how their students inspire one another, and what and how students learn from one another, without being constrained by adult notions of what makes a picture successful, of what works and what doesn't.

As students leaned, sat, or sprawled along the main hall of the building, as they looked or sketched in silence, a visitor remarked in passing, "This looks like the Met [Metropolitan Museum of Art]! What are they doing?" The students were engaged in an activity that used draw-

"I think it would be great to go to an art museum because it would give us lots of ideas"

ing and writing for authentic purposes: thinking, under-standing, seeing. Students were gaining new ideas and perspectives on other students by focusing on the work of their community of peers.

The all-school exhibitions also allowed adults to in-teract with students in an educated, meaningful way. Care-fully planned displays of children's work can make a school like a museum, with "the potential to engage students, to teach them, to stimulate their understanding, and most important, to help them assume responsibility for their own future learning" (Gardner, p. 202). Our exhibitions led to a more informed community, which broadened the conversation about the role of arts in literacy. Parents' un-derstanding led to enthusiastic and ongoing support of the program. By extending the learning into the hallways, our exhibitions extended the classroom community, expanded the learning, and included evaluation, reflection, commu-nication, collaboration, and authentic learning on the part of the teacher, other adults, and students.

At The Art Students League in New York City the class I was in sat in a circle. A large drawing pad tilted on my lap. I concen-trated on the models in the center of the circle as they settled into a pose for twenty minutes. I focused on the top of the head, the eyes; my pen wandered slowly, deliberately on the page as I began to imagine it touching the shoulder, the arm. I only occasionally glanced down at the figure forming on the paper. This was an ex-ercise in learning how to see, a skill all artists need. "Change," the voice of the instructor rang out as the model rested before tak-ing the next pose.

Early in my teaching career, an artist neighbor encouraged me to study art as an adult. The attention of my kindergarten teacher had perhaps initiated my desire to be an artist. The image of my neighbor sitting out by the marsh creek, glancing at the flag waving in the distance and drawing it with pen and ink, was part of an apprenticeship that encouraged me to follow my own desire to be an artist.

Apprenticeships for Learning

Students sat with drawing boards tilted from their laps to the table. Their eyes were focused on the models, a stuffed horse, lion, rag doll, bear. Their hands guided the pen on the white paper; they tried to imagine their pen touching the edges of the model. The room was silent except for an occasional giggle or sigh. "Rest," I called out as I moved into the circle, lifted the stuffed horse from its former position to a new one while the students clipped a clean piece of paper to their board. They saved all the drawings, even the mistakes, in their portfolios. After every pose the students held up their drawings to show their progress in seeing. Trevor drew the lion from the back, Jane drew it from the front. Allen drew the lion and the bear posing together, from three different angles (see Figure 3–9).

The silence continued later when my younger students met the same challenge: George drew the horse standing on his back legs. Thomas, grade one, drew a view of the horse from the back (see Figure 3–10). Dennis drew the bear and the monkey from the side. When she came to pick up her class, a kindergarten teacher asked, "How did you teach perspective in one hour?" I explained we were learning how to see, because observation is essential to what real artists and writers do. This activity as well as many other factors—the environment of the classroom, my use of language, and my attempt to "do what real artists do"—were part of my students' constant immersion in apprenticeship.

Student writing about this "seeing" activity showed me that they had gained confidence in their own drawing, had learned the importance of looking at the model, and had noticed their classmates while they worked. A second grader responded, "I discovered the more I look at the horse the better I draw." Another wrote, "When I saw people drawing I thought the pen guided them." A third grader wrote: "I drew today. It was fun. . . . I like having my pen glide across the paper and [having] something you're proud of at the end. It's like the feel of the waves going

FIGURE 3–9
Allen's three views of a lion and bear.

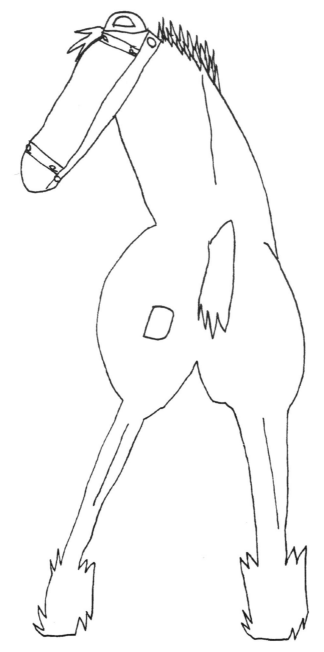

FIGURE 3–10
Thomas's rear view of a horse.

across the paper." Jessica drew two views of the horse and wrote poetically how it felt to experience the activity: "I saw my sketch as the creation of light. It felt as though I was floating in space, waiting to be caught by my sketch. A sketch is not a sketch, it is your feeling, your thought, and your mind put together."

Howard Gardner says that through an apprenticeship "novices have the opportunity to witness on a daily basis the reasons for various skills, procedures, concepts, and symbolic notational systems" (p. 203). In the artists workshop apprenticeship did not mean that I was master, but that I was a role model of art skills and aesthetic attitudes, that I embodied artistic practices.

In our artists workshop students observed my inquiry as an artist as I worked on my own pictures and collages or sketched them while they worked. They would find me writing in my journal if they came to the art room early in the morning or if they noticed me sitting outside while they played on the playground during recess. Just as the distant memory of my kindergarten teacher had come to influence what I did as a teacher, my neighbor had modeled the world of an artist for me and inspired me to reach for my own role as an artist. A teacher's own literate behavior can make for an informal apprenticeship, and can have enormous influence on students' learning.

In her study of the influence of apprenticeships on creative individuals, Vera John-Steiner refers to Chomsky's description of the important contrast between formal ways of acquiring knowledge in a discipline and informal methods of apprenticeship. Play and creative environments "may contribute to the fluency and ease in the work of some creative individuals" (p. 41). Our classroom environment included signs labeled "Studio," "Gallery," and "Portfolio" to help us focus on thinking of it as an artists studio. Art reproductions and quotations on the blackboard by artists and writers gave students the legacy "of distant teachers" (p. 37). The opportunity to participate as ap-

FIGURE 3–11
Kevin's boat.

prentices in the artists workshop enabled my students to learn and interpret in many ways.

Kevin worked hard on his fat boat done in bright markers (see Figure 3–11), and I asked him what inspired his picture. "That guy over there," he responded. My eyes followed the line made by his pointed finger to a Monet reproduction pinned to the board in the Gallery, which surrounded this class of first graders as they worked. Dennis, a second grader, did his version of Georgia O'Keeffe's red poppy (see Plate 8), while Alicia, a fourth grader, used crayons to make a picture influenced by a work by Rousseau. Christina painted a picture inspired by Redon, while I responded to Joyce's picture of flowers by suggesting it was Matisse-like. The artists whose creations surrounded the work area were integral to our rehearsal conversations. Students were inspired and influenced by these artists, their "distant teachers," as they chose their own topics and learned technique at their own pace. The works (and words) of these artists provided a means for students to think, see, model technique, and open their imagination. They gave students ideas for picture making, promoted an awareness of a range of interpretations, and helped emphasize that there are many realities, not just one.

Becky, a second grader, was inspired by Monet, and painted a picture of poppies. She explained, "I see beautiful flowers and I can feel the wind, I can hear the trees going side to side." Through looking at and discussing the work of artists, students like Becky were moved by the arts, learned how to talk about the arts, and through authentically engaging in the arts learned how to be released into their own streams of consciousness.

Well-known artists and writers helped me demonstrate the importance of the thinking behind pictures and the ways pictures can be expressive. This helped students to relax about the appearance of their pictures. After a class of third graders silently scanned Kandinsky's "Improvisation," they responded to my question "What do you see?"

"Scribbles," "a palette," "designs," "a dream," "a leopard," "into the mind," "swirling rainbows," "red," "yellow," "blue," "green," "black."

When I asked, "What do you think about as you look at this work?" they responded, "Goes in a circle," "looks like music," "an alley," "thinking like in a panic."

Discussing the works of artists and constantly asking students to think about a picture they've made can help lead students to connections in thinking, to words, to meanings. By asking students to look, notice, and think about what they see, we can empower students to depend on their own vision.

Through conversation, demonstrations of technique, and teacher modeling, students can learn to look further, focusing on line, brushwork, color, image, and composition. Jake, a fourth grader, pulled his stool back to the Gallery to copy a poster from a van Gogh retrospective. He explained that he learned about how to make things look like they were "going back" in the picture (see Figure 3–12). Kindergartner pictures, versions of flowers in vases (see Figure 3–13), were influenced by Redon as well as the displayed work of older students. Emma wrote in her notebook: "Today I made a blue flower. It took a lot of time making the right color. I got my idea from Vincent van Gogh and his field." James wrote, "I got some of my ideas from the impressionists. The others I dreamed in my mind."

Just as literature provided models in the writers workshop, the work of artists in the artists workshop provided students with models for technique and style; these models prompted students to learn at their own pace, even to advance beyond prescribed descriptions of age-appropriate technique. As the workshop developed, the pictures, words, and conversations of the students helped me further understand the importance of bringing the arts into literacy and confirmed that "both producing and perceiving art require the ability to process and manipulate symbols and to make extremely subtle discriminations"

FIGURE 3–12
Jake's copy of a van Gogh.

FIGURE 3–13
A vase of flowers inspired by Redon.

(Winner, p. 12). The students' encounters and explorations in making and thinking led them to think about their involvement with various forms of art, thus expanding the idea of literacy beyond reading and writing to making pictures and studying the work of artists. This opened more doors through which children could participate in constructing meaning and offered new ways of understanding, seeing, and self-expression. Karen Gallas, a first-grade teacher, writes, "For both teacher and child, the arts offer an expanded notion of classroom discourse that is not solely grounded in linear objective language and thinking, but rather recognizes the full range of human potential for expressions and understanding" (p. 42).

Artists and writers must be ever present in the artists workshop, inspiring, providing distant apprenticeships, and influencing student pictures and thinking. Teachers also need to engage in the world of their discipline, to provide an apprenticeship through modeling, to engage in literate behavior, and to encourage students to interact with the environment of the classroom. The arts need to be an integral part of the curriculum, part of emerging literacy along with reading and writing. It is through formal and informal apprenticeships, near and distant teachers, that children learn to work toward being creative individuals.

End Piece

One Friday, during my last class, the principal brought a parent who was shopping for a new school to the art room. I greeted the visitor at the door, a group of first graders serving as backdrop. Before taking any time to notice what was happening in the classroom, she asked, "What do you believe in art?" I understood her to be inquiring about my philosophy of teaching.

Stunned, I responded haltingly. I couldn't answer that question quickly. Just then her eyes shifted from me to the students, dressed in their huge smocks, hard at work on their projects. I knew the topics of their conversations, the intensity of their work.

"What assignment did you give them?" she asked. "My goodness, they are working so hard!"

"I didn't give them an assignment," I responded. "They are doing their own work."

This parent too learned by observing, asking questions based on what she saw, as I had done. Words do not always provide enough of an explanation for any of us.

I returned to the workshop, my own smock spattered with the paint of my own projects. I settled next to Kevin, who was concentrating on a drawing done with markers. I described what had just happened.

"What do *you* think my beliefs are about teaching art?" I asked him.

Kevin looked at the pocket of my smock, on which I had drawn a heart around "Miss Ernst," then up to my face. "You believe in imagination," he said. Without any self-consciousness, his eyes wandered back to his work and he returned to his drawing. The question—and I—had seemingly disappeared.

The parent who visited that day had briefly observed the workshop in progress, a classroom community where the students and the teacher were involved in their own projects and learning. She saw what may have appeared to be a simple picture. In fact, it was a workshop of learning layered with many components critical to the experience within. It was based on a writers workshop approach, but here the visual was a part of the emerging literacy, and writing and reading were essential to picture making, meaning making, and learning.

The concept of teacher as observer is an important one. It helped me move beyond my vision of what this workshop could be, to listen to the conversations, read the writing, observe the students as they worked, ask questions, and record my students' understanding. Through observing, going inside the pictures and the thinking of my students, I began to understand how the experiences within the workshop worked together to form a community of learning.

Creating a classroom community where the teacher and students are involved with their own steps forward as learners, and where many ways of meaning making are honored, was both the focus of and the source of the energy behind all that went on here. Maxine Greene (1991) writes:

> We ought to reach out to establish ateliers, studios, places where music can be composed and rehearsed, where poems and stories can be read. There might be new collaborations among questioners, as teachers and students both engage in perceptual journeys, grasp works and words and events in contexts of meaning, undertake common searches for their place and significance in a history to which they too belong and which they invent and interpret as they live. (pp. 38–39)

In my perceptual journey, my role as observer helped me understand the inventions and the interpretations of my students as the artists workshop evolved.

✿ I need poetry books. — I can read some "short poems" and they can create a picture or collage to "tell it" I need music — we can create a painting to the music.

Chosen in black and green, pencil and crayons, drawing Zuckerman's Farm... in Charlotte's Webb.

4

Moving Inside

TEACHER AS OBSERVER, STUDENTS AS INFORMANTS

I announced to my eighth-grade class, "I am leaving. I am taking my journal to the corner of this room and I will be watching you for the next five days to understand how you approach writers workshop without me. I want you to depend on each other for conferencing, to use your time for writing and revising." Discouraged because after many months of the workshop I felt my eighth graders were depending too much on my conferencing and advising skills, I decided to pull back and watch my own classroom at work. I wanted to develop a community of independent writers where collaboration was integral. During those five days, when my students and I could not interact, I learned that Jeff needed time to stare out the window to find a topic, that the arrangement of the desks did not provide a place where students could write in silence, and that when students were engaged in their own writing or conferring they could ignore others' behavior.

Observing was at the heart of both my writing workshop and my artists workshop. I reflected each day in my journal, and in the beginning I focused on my vision, on what I wanted to occur in the classroom, what book or art reproduction I would choose for rehearsal, or what tool or technique I would demonstrate. I knew from my experience as a teacher-researcher in my writers workshop that teaching is more than establishing a routine or giving a performance. As I got to know the students and felt more comfortable, I found that my observations helped me slow down and begin raising questions about my students' work. Nancie Atwell (1987b) suggests that becoming an observer helps us stop focusing on presenting a lesson and evaluating its results and start observing our students in the process of learning, listening to what they can tell us, and responding as they need us. This, she says, helps the classroom become a community in which teacher and students are partners in inquiry.

As I drew my students in my journal I captured their poses, what they were working on, and which media they used. I drew Ellen and Emma as they sat with their feet tucked under them, white, wrinkled smocks hiding their tiny figures as they sketched a rag doll. I noticed that markers, crayons, and palettes of paint were their tools of learning, and that their collaboration was significant. When I drew Carol as she mixed saucers of new colors using the primary colors in her palette, I remembered that I needed to allow time for discovery. As Kelly and Janet joined me at the Writing Center, I noticed it was hard for Kelly to "make words," as she kept looking over at Janet's paper. I remembered the value of giving time to every step toward literacy, in reading, writing, or picturing. When Ellen asked for Wite-Out because she "ruined her painting," I wondered if my students were revising pictures as they revised writing, using both as forms of expression and meaning. Observing my students at work drew me to them and helped me learn about the meaning behind their creation. I reached a new understanding about my vision for the workshop, and about the role of collaboration, writing, and making pictures as complementary learning processes.

Drawing helped me to look closely at students and to question more intently what they were doing. I captured Brendan in his smock; as I did so I noticed his new attempt at painting. Up to this point in the year Brendan had worked rapidly, mostly painting in swirls and lines. This day he was engaged for a longer time; when I asked why, he said that he felt this painting was different from other paintings he had done. When I asked whether any of the paintings we had looked at in rehearsal that day had given him any ideas, he answered yes, then walked down to the sharing area and pointed to a series of flowers by Maria, a fourth grader, which were inspired by O'Keeffe. "That one," he said. While close observation led me to notice my students' small steps of progress in their picture making, questioning led me to understand the influence both artists and older students had on them. Individual responses showed me which aspects of their vision were at work. Art, artists, collaboration, and response were important. My teaching and continued questioning grew out of my detailed observations. Looking at the students' pictures I could see progress, I could praise their use of technique and media. However, it became clear to me almost immediately that studying their pictures from the outside would not unveil the depth and complexity that I knew were there.

Brendan's smock. covers him all the way past his knees — his Dad's T-shirt transformed.

"I've been standing outside my paintings. I have to get inside them somehow," Jackson told his friend in *Jackson Makes His Move* (Glass). By asking my students to "go inside" their pictures and thinking, I was able to learn the significance of what I saw. Matt, a fourth grader, looked long and hard at his pastel painting of a river and trees (see Plate 3); then he began to write, to describe what he would find if he went inside his painting:

> The flowers and leaves sway
> as the wind
> gently blows.
> The sun brightens
> The gleam from the river
> as the clouds float away.
> A bird chirps and then I
> know.
> Know that I'm safe here.

Observing helped me raise questions, and I found answers by collecting students' writing and conducting informal and formal interviews. The writing and the interviews helped me get inside the drawings in my own research journal, inside the pictures of my students, and inside the picture of the workshop. It was on the inside that the interplay of imagination and craft happened, a fact the students' writing disclosed. My younger students began teaching me to take risks and to understand more about their thinking, their intentions, their meanings, about how they integrated pictures and words. It was only by going inside the pictures and the thinking that I began to learn how this workshop was a workshop of learning, how the visual was a partner with the verbal.

No More Orange Snakes

The younger students, especially the kindergartners, kept me off balance from the beginning. They presented the biggest challenge that first day, when Anna sat on my lap crying while I read *Mouse Paint,* and later when, as a result of my attempt to collaborate with their teacher, her fellow kindergartners made what looked like orange snakes instead of pumpkins. I failed to connect the work to my students' abilities and intentions. It was my research that helped me to note the gradations in their learning and to use those nuances to learn more about my artists workshop.

A line on the "Permissions" sign dangling over the sink in the room read, "It is OK to wait until you feel ready." My third and fourth graders helped me feel ready to learn about my younger students. With a background in secondary education, I knew little of the possibilities of writing and learning in the primary grades. Just as the memory of my eighth graders informed what I did with the third and fourth graders, the work of my new older students helped me consider how my younger students related words and pictures. With journal in hand I stepped inside the kindergarten and first-grade workshops.

Kindergartners drew houses. Many were big, others were small, but there was always the glimpse of a yellow sun. I saw the wide range of influences in their pictures, from imagined monsters (see Figure 4–1) to duplications of French impressionist paintings. As I walked around the room it became clear to me that the literature I read to them and the work of older students had strongly influenced their pictures. The kindergartners told me the stories of their pictures, asked me to write on them, and taught me about the connections between their words and their pictures.

I listened to their serious conversations as they worked in the studio. "I am making my father," declared Jennifer, as she pointed to the brilliant-colored shape of a man.

Felicia said, "I am making Alice and Wonderland," and another student asked, "Our Alice?"

"No."

"I read that."

"Hey, red and blue makes purple!"

I learned that their seemingly disconnected conversations were connected to their literacy, since they had not yet learned to separate reading, writing, and picture making. Their pictures were stories, their work was discovery, and they were influenced by literature, by older students, and by artists.

When I asked Bruce what his picture was, he responded, "It's a fire truck . . . going to a fire." Alex told me about his picture, called "Proud," inspired by *Jackson Makes His Move*.

"There's a blue sun and there is the yellow shining down. A girl is throwing a ball on the ground and she is jumping up in the air. That is a thing that is cutting the grass. If you walk to this little ladder you'll walk across—shoot across—and fall into greenish yellow and mix up to blue." Melinda's painting of broad bands of blue and green prompted me to ask her the same questions I had posed earlier to my third and fourth graders: What do you see?

FIGURE 4–1
A kindergartner's imagined monster.

feel? What title would you give the picture? Her responses became the words to accompany her picture (see Figure 4–2). Having described his painting as "a space alien," Bob revised his words to "a Chinese space alien and his home is made out of a rock."

Some students began writing on their own pictures. Jennifer said, "I forgot to write something," asked me for my pen, and wrote, "SULA RAINBOW." As we were finishing class she wrote "KIMBERBERLY" after many trips to the sink to ask Kimberly how to spell her name. My younger students were graciously helping my cautious learning, their words and pictures were partners. Their conversations convinced me to give each of the kindergarten through second-grade classes an artists notebook. At the end of class they discussed their discoveries while I recorded them on a large sketch pad of newsprint. They began linking words to their discoveries and at times answered my questions about their process.

"Our table discovered new colors: dark black and hot pink."

"Colors change to other colors."

"Jessica and I have been asking each other what we want to make."

The artists workshop of my younger students included invention, surprise, collaboration, and more. Kindergartners told me many interesting things.

"When the paint is dry you can paint over it."

"When you mix a color you don't like, you can add in another color."

"More turns to a mess."

My younger students were showing me the meaning behind Ruth Hubbard's important study of first graders, *Authors of Pictures, Draughtsmen of Words*, which describes how children use both verbal and visual languages to help them sort out, understand, and cope with their world. Hubbard writes, "Drawing is not just for children who can't yet write fluently, and creating pictures is not just part of rehearsal for writing. Images at any age are part of

The Trip

I'm on a boat
    going someplace
On a cold windy day
Blue sky
Big green meadow
Bluish green water
The trip.

FIGURE 4–2
Melinda's painting and subsequent poem.

PICTURING LEARNING

FIGURE 4–3
Anna's painting.

the serious business of making meaning—partners with words for communicating inner designs" (p. 157).

Through the words of my younger students, I began to understand their discovery in learning. When a first-grade teacher came to the room to pick up her class, she announced, "My kids don't know where writing ends and art begins." I smiled, thinking how both art and writing were essential to the learning here, theirs and mine. Anna, who entered the workshop on the first day, crying, "I can't draw, I can't draw," became a painter (see Figure 4–3). Her classmates painted their feelings while urging me to write their stories.

The kindergartners filed into the workshop each week, their eyes wandering through the room looking at the work in progress. After rehearsal, they told me what they planned to work on and moved to the tables to work. Two students passed out the big white sheets of paper on which stories and pictures would develop. One day, Emma asked if she could have her portfolio to finish a picture she started last time and opened her portfolio to show me the beginning of a blue collage, explaining that she intended to finish it after she completed her painting.

Over time my younger students informed me that they were thinking ahead, planning their projects, making choices and connections in the workshop. The "Permissions" sign above the sink also read, "It is OK to try something you don't know. It is OK to find your own pace." It was listening, asking, observing, and going inside the pictures of my younger students that enabled me to make subtle changes. It was my work as a researcher that freed me to expand their choices. There were no more orange snakes; now there were stories, pictures, and a deeper understanding of their learning.

Alice So Far   Alice stood at her table. Her big smock with "Alice" written on the back slipped off her shoulder. Working intently, she dotted the paint onto her paper, stepped back, looked,

Alice stands at her table, smock slipping off the red-shirted left shoulder. She concentrates almost like an orchestra leader - she dabs the paint onto her paper - looks - steps back a little and then continues. She brings it over and says "This is my best painting so far."

then continued. As I passed her table, she remarked to me, "This is my best painting so far."

Alice was influenced by authors and artists; after listening to Tomie dePaola's *The Legend of the Indian Paintbrush*, she went directly to her table to make "an Indian from her imagination." Writing about her in my journal that day I noted that Monet and the impressionists influenced her as she dotted paint to make flowers, or boldly let her brush strokes become grass, mountains, and sky (one of her landscapes is shown in Figure 4–4). Alice influenced others and was admired by her classmates. "What do you think of my picture, Alice?" a classmate asked as he approached her table, seeking her opinion. Marla, who sat at Alice's table, learned by listening to Alice talk about her pictures and by watching Alice experiment with media. Alice, a first grader, was Marla's teacher. "The animal picture, a leopard hiding in the bushes" was her favorite picture (see Plate 11), made with "strokes going up and down," as she described in her portfolio review. She liked "the sky, the grass, and the flowers that hide him." She was conscious of how she created her pictures, and remembered the details of most of the ones in her portfolio. Her portrait of Gerald, a classmate, was one of her favorites. "I used magic markers, different colors." She easily gave advice to others while crediting her classmates with inspiring her work. The leopard picture came to her as "Dennis, in my class, was drawing a picture of a leopard and I decided to make my own." She decided that "the leopard should be in the woods."

Alice's mother enthusiastically described how Alice practiced drawing at home, requested art supplies for gifts, and moved beyond what her mother could imagine her doing. Alice was involved in an apprenticeship both in school and at home. She constantly attempted to do what she saw me doing, drawing my students at work. One day she drew a picture of a visitor to our class. She often put herself into positions to help her understand a pose before she drew. In her portfolio review she explained, "I like to do sketches

FIGURE 4–4
Alice's landscape influenced by the impressionists.

of people in ballet positions. I put myself in a ballet position, see how I look and feel and then draw the person."

Alice was the first student to hand me a picture, a cut-paper collage. She said, "Here, Miss Ernst, this is for you." Her gift, her intensity as she worked, and her attempts to emulate me made me realize that apprenticeship was important for her just as it had been for me in my kindergarten class. Sharing my work in writing and drawing showed me how modeling can teach in countless ways, helping students draw beyond their grade or age.

"I think I've changed, really," Alice explained in an interview. "In kindergarten I wasn't good." She had learned to "use more detail," she said, and haltingly added, "My classmates admire me." She was inspired by artists, illustrators, and other students, while she inspired them through her serious work as an emerging first-grade artist. Like most artists, Alice concentrated on her pictures, worked the paint into a picture, and constantly stepped back to observe the developing work. She was at once part of the creation and the observer of the process. Her comment about her work "so far" showed me that her present painting was part of a continuing process of creating and learning.

Being an observer in my own classroom freed me to see the emerging workshop from a distance, just as Alice did with her own pictures. Closely observing students like Alice helped me examine the elements of my vision at work in the classroom. Alice exemplified the influence of art and literature in making pictures and the importance of apprenticeship. Considered an expert by others, Alice modeled while showing that even when different abilities are present, collaboration and response from peers are integral to creating a community of learners.

Carl Creating: Antic and Serious

Carl walked across the art room, held up a picture he had just finished, and asked, "What do you think, Miss Ernst?" I glanced at the bottom of the page and noticed his signature: Carl van Gogh. I responded, "The question is, what do you think of your picture?"

He smiled and said, "I love it." Carl continued to sign his work using the "van Gogh" surname and throughout the year taught me about the role of writing and pictures, and the importance of ownership, artists, illustrators, and self-image in this workshop of learning. His answers often surprised me as much as his signature had, reminding me how important it is that students feel confident in their work, and that this workshop was about more than just pictures. He convinced me that I should not stop with observations, or draw conclusions from what I saw. I needed to ask questions, to go inside and learn the intentions of students.

Carl was a fourth grader. His works included a drawing of the tree outside the school (see Figure 4–5); "Paradise in the Jungle"; and "A River of Life" (see Plate 4). His favorite works were "The Musketeer" (see Figure 4–6), "Boy Watching the Comet at the Water's Edge," and "Paradise Painting in Progress." He liked most to work with watercolor, and generally liked "the way my pictures look." He always seemed to know what he was going to do when he approached his table. He appreciated "getting to choose to draw whatever I want."

Carl always sat facing the door that opened to the outside. Three of his friends often sat with him, and they talked quietly while they worked. Throughout the year, Carl was open to answering my questions. If I asked what a picture was about he would respond thoughtfully and deliberately.

"Paradise," he said, then corrected himself. "This is paradise in the jungle. This is a waterfall." He made sure his answers were accurate. In his portfolio review his mother wrote, "Carl says the drawing is right on the tips of his fingers ready to come out or on the page waiting to be drawn." Carl and his friends at the table balanced seriousness and play as they worked and discussed their art over the year. When I sat down to interview Carl, he shifted be-

FIGURE 4–5
Carl's drawing of a tree.

PICTURING LEARNING

FIGURE 4–6
"The Musketeer" by Carl.

(Van Gogh)
always sets
Facing the door to the outside and he always
seems to know what he is going to work on.
Watching him makes me realize how much
I understand after I interviewed him that
day. Today I will sit and watch

tween looking at me and glancing out the window. Jake, a friend at the table, said, "In our last art class we are going to have a masterpiece duel."

Earlier in the year I had drawn Carl in my journal as he leaned over his artists notebook working on a poem and a sketch. I observed at the time that he was working on writing while other students had already begun to paint or draw their picture projects. In his interview, I asked him about the painting that went with the poem he had written in his notebook months before (see Figure 4–7). He explained it was not a poem, or even writing to go with a painting he had made, but notes he had taken for a picture he had imagined and wanted to remember. He did not have enough time to paint it that day. He explained, "I knew I was going to paint it later on. It was like a reminder. I didn't really mean it to be a poem . . . but I guess it is one. If I wanted to add some things, my poem would remind me of a bunch of different things to stick in . . . and the quick little messy sketches . . . they helped." He explained thoughtfully, "After I finished a painting that day I was thinking about my next painting. I looked outside, saw all trees, the leaves falling off . . . and thought of a forest, nature and all that. I got inspired by nature stuff." He looked out the window, his cheeks flushed as he thought; then he continued. "And I had a pure image of it in my head. I could imagine it like a finished painting. And I thought it would be a great idea."

Carl used writing to record "a pure image," while the quick sketches helped fill in the details. He came in during recess that week to paint the picture from the notes he had written, transforming the finished painting in his head to one on paper (again, see Plate 4). I asked him to rewrite the words from his notebook to accompany the picture. He did, adding some poetry-type line breaks:

> A river of life
> with no man and
> pure peace in the wilderness.

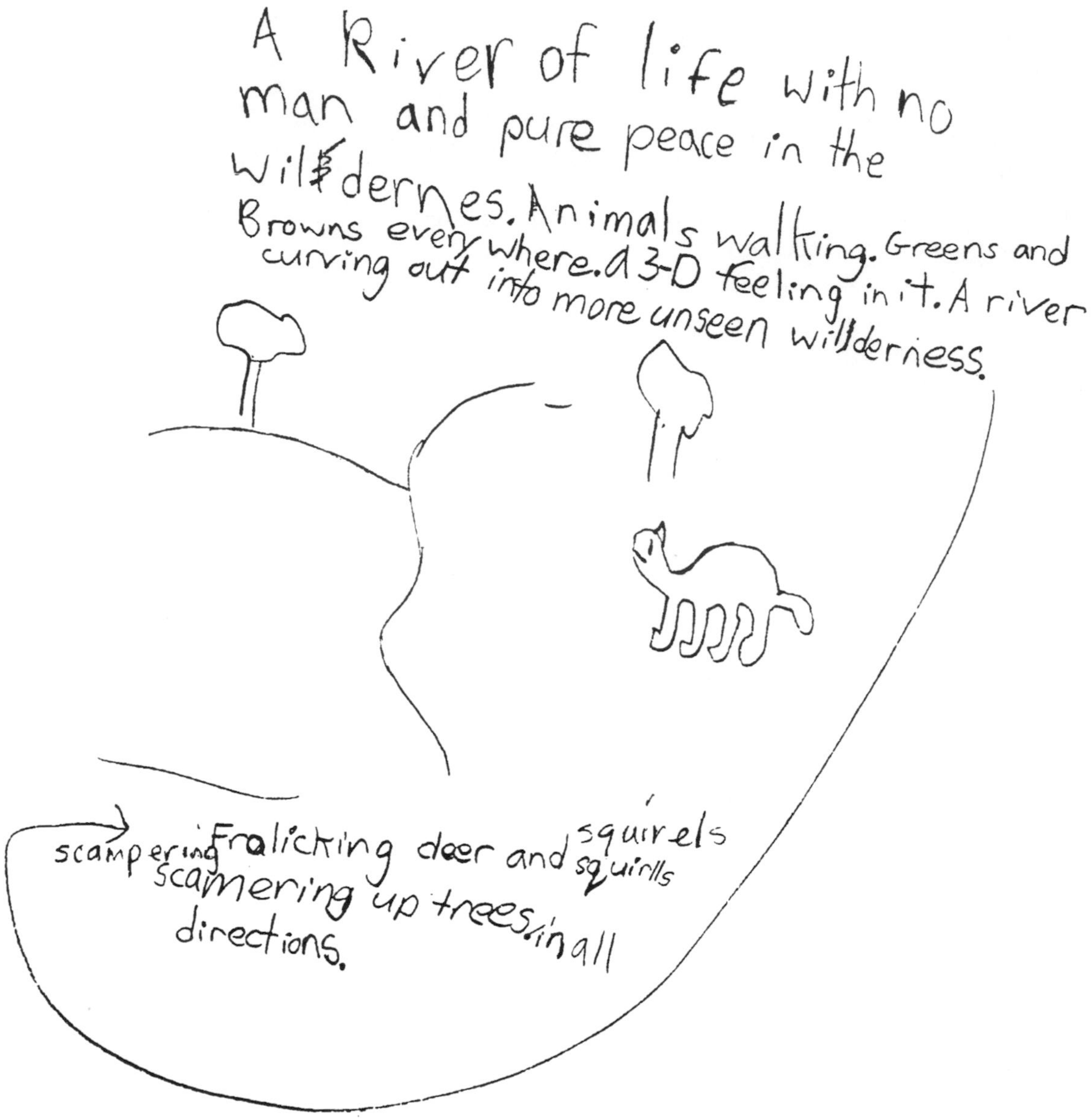

FIGURE 4–7
Carl's notes for a painting that became his "A River of Life."

Animals walking.
Greens and browns everywhere.
A 3-D feeling in it.
A river curving
out into more unseen wilderness.
Frolicking deer and squirrels
   scampering
up trees in all directions.

My initial observation of Carl leaning over his notebook taught me that when the workshop is open to students' own projects and to many forms of expression, some
students will choose to write while others paint; some may
even look at books to gather ideas. Carl showed me the importance of asking further, of not drawing conclusions from
observation alone. Through our discussions, I learned that
Carl wrote in words the images he saw in his mind and
then created the picture from those words. My students
were not just writing about pictures; they were finding
ways to let their writing and picture making work together.
My observation could not stop with looking. I needed to
go inside my observations; to sit with my students to ask
their intentions; to learn. And so I was able to take the
workshop beyond my vision.

In his artists notebook, Carl had commented on the
detailed drawing of a tree outside the classroom (Figure
4–5). "I felt happy about finally being allowed to draw that
tree. I found that I have a talent for sketching." I sat down
next to Carl after I read that comment, fully expecting him
to be hard at work on his incredible tree drawing, but I
found him working instead on "Dracula in Reebok Sneakers"! He continued to draw a river going through a grave-
yard while I asked him why he wasn't going to finish the
tree. "That's the problem with me in art. I am very impa-
tient. . . . I only need to finish the bark."

I was initially disappointed, but Carl answered a
question I had wondered about earlier in the year: What
role does experimenting or relaxing play in our process?

There is a necessary rhythm in creating. Carl couldn't work on this meticulous line drawing of a tree forever. He had to have fun, play, experiment, feel free; that is what Dracula did for him. How often as teachers do we stop our students or ourselves from that play? How often do we disrupt that rhythm? We must strike a balance in our work in the classroom between serious and antic. In his interview, I asked Carl about the phrase in his artists notebook, about "finally being allowed to draw that tree." Carl explained how he had wanted to draw the tree when he was younger. "It looked so big . . . out of my imagination. . . . I always wanted to draw that tree and rock but never had enough time." Now Carl was in charge of his projects, selecting his own topics, creating his own schedule, and finding a rhythm for his work.

In his artists notebook Carl wrote, "The art room makes me feel confident in what I'm doing. It influences me to make something nice on the paper, the pictures around the room do that to me." Carl explained that his inspiration came from "the Gallery mostly because I am sitting next to it." His words, pictures, and answers confirmed for me the importance of the environment and the ways that inspirations inside and outside the classroom can influence students' work.

Carl volunteered, "I have the exact whole picture in my mind before I draw—like Mozart, he had the whole song in his head before he put the notes on the staff." He explained that he knew about Mozart because he had done a report on him the year before. He reiterated how his work came from an image in his head or, as he described in his portfolio review, "I just close my eyes and think of words that bring an image to my mind." Carl's response to my last question, whether and how he had changed over the year, confirmed what I noticed about him that first time he had signed his work Carl van Gogh: "Most definitely. I've gotten a lot better and as I said a lot more confident in my work."

I had followed Carl with interest throughout the year, drawing him at work, reading his artists notebook, asking him questions. I was always surprised. He taught me about the possible inaccuracy of hasty conclusions, the importance of pace, the mix between stretching and playing, and the ability to continue to create. When he signed his work Carl van Gogh, I saw what it meant to really believe in one's work, to step beyond meeting someone else's standards of approval. Carl's use of writing led me to wonder about the many ways students used writing in the artists workshop and pointed to other connections between the visual and verbal.

Christina: More Than Magic

I thought of Christina as my artist in residence. Her smock was always covered with splashes of paint and streaks of marker. She made almost daily visits to the workshop, to experiment with color and shapes and to use a combination of materials. She seemed to go deep into herself as she worked; and she did hundreds of pieces throughout the year. They included a vase of flowers inspired by the artist Redon (see the cover of this book), a Leo Lionni–style collage (see Plate 6), landscapes, sketches, abstract designs, more. Christina represented the vision I had always had of what it means to be an artist. Her total immersion in her work and her ability to expand and explore her own margins caused me to envy her enough to begin my own exploration in crayon and watercolor. Christina inspired me as an artist. In the art room she was an expert.

All of this success was in contrast to other parts of her school day. Christina had been born in Brazil, and her native language was Portuguese; she had great difficulty reading and writing in English. She was supported through a tutorial program and enjoyed a close relationship with her tutor, with whom she met daily. I watched her throughout the year and was inspired by the quality of her pictures. I wondered about the role of art in her learning, and

Christina she looks up down up down
drawing with her left hand—
Right hand propped lightly
on her clip board. a flood of
memories come as I watch—
her apron, short smock, crying,
her "favorite subject." Are these the
important stories— why does the
writing click most w/ 4th grade?

I saw how she seemed to use it successfully as another language.

On the afternoon Christina came to the art room to be interviewed, she was accompanied by her friend Maria. I read aloud from their artists notebooks, beginning with Maria's: "Art is magic." In our conversation, Christina described what Maria's statement meant to her. She began, "The piece of paper is white, and if you do anything on it . . . um . . . it still looks . . . pretty . . . because it's something you never drew . . . and you think, wow, that's so pretty. Especially your first picture, you thought it was ugly, then you show your mother and it was like . . . this is magic."

Further questioning revealed that Christina had taken home a picture early in the year and showed it to her mother, who responded, "That's magic. You used to draw sloppy. You can be an artist someday if you keep dreaming." Christina concluded, "And I thought art was magic."

I asked Christina for advice about what I should retain in the workshop in future years. She emphasized that I should "let them draw what they want. You let us have choices. . . . Do you want to paint, do collage? Do you want to do this or that? You make it make more sense to us. When I'm here it makes me want to draw. I say you can choose what you want to do. Art just makes me do something better, makes me think about something, and just let it out on a piece of paper. And that's what I think art's all about."

In art Christina experienced a new confidence and a feeling of success. This was clearly depicted in the quality of her pictures and in the admiration she received from her classmates. She felt she had changed as an artist over the year. "I kind of . . . I was drawing sloppier and when I was coloring them the color was going out of them. But now I don't need a pencil or anything, I just paint what's in my mind and it comes out. It comes out prettier than I ever thought."

While valuing the comments and praise of her mother, Christina appreciated the honest feedback she received from her friends as she worked. "You've got to have friends to kind of tell you how it really looks. If you show it to your mother she'll probably say, 'Oh, that's a beautiful thing.' Here your friends will tell you what's real, what you've really done, and if it's not good you'll try again." Even an extremely quiet student like Christina, one who appeared to work alone, found collaboration and response essential to her progress as an artist.

Christina demonstrated how making pictures and doing well in one subject could influence performance in other subjects. As Christina's tutor began to realize the importance and success Christina found in art, she let Christina use picture making to express herself. "For math I can do a picture and before I never did that," Christina said. She went on to explain how she told her tutor about her work during the day. "Sometimes I don't say to her out of my mouth . . . I draw it down on the paper. . . . She will think about it. And sometimes I draw the little lines . . . she'll notice . . . she hangs them up . . . it looks like I'm special to her. It makes me feel better." As art became an essential part of Christina's whole learning she made progress in small ways, noticed only through close observation. Even though writing in her artists notebook was difficult for her, she began to use invented spelling to write her ideas. Pictures provided Christina with a way of communicating with her tutor and a way into her whole learning. We often think students who have difficulty in learning need specific, step-by-step directions, but the workshop approach in art seemed to allow Christina to tap into her own ideas, her own expertise. She looked forward to her weekly art class, reinforced by her almost daily visits during recess. Artists workshop provided Christina with the success she needed to approach math, reading, and writing. She was excited as she came to the workshop, where she was an expert. Pictures helped Christina make meaning and express herself. From my perspective, making pictures and the artists workshop were more than magic for Christina.

Unfortunately, this was not a perspective held or understood by others. With the recommendation of her classroom teacher and the agreement of her parents, Christina was scheduled to be placed in a special school for children with learning disabilities and physical impairment. When I heard that this might happen in Christina's fifth-grade year, I appealed to the principal and the placement committee. I was dismayed that the opinion of the "special" teacher had not been asked, especially in the class where Christina had spent so much time and had met with such success. This experience made me realize how urgent it was to take away the title of "special" and the idea that the arts are marginal activities.

Art provided Christina with a way of knowing. Further work in it could have expanded her literacy. Regardless of that, Christina began her fifth-grade year in the special school.

Jessica: Picture of Wonders

On the day I intended to interview Jessica about her work, especially the way she combined words and pictures, she wrote in her artists notebook, "Miss Ernst, please read what I wrote today. Jessica." She then continued, "Miss Ernst has helped me see what I really am."

Jessica, a fourth grader, always seemed to bounce into the art room. Her line drawing of a horse with the accompanying writing in her notebook ("A sketch is not a sketch") had prompted me to inquire about the process of making pictures as described in writing. Her fourth-grade teacher frequently came to observe his students at work in the art room and often watched Jessica because, he said, she wrote more and with more sensitivity in the artists workshop than she did in her writers workshop in his classroom.

Her torn-paper dinosaur (see Figure 4–8) was an example of the whimsy and speed in her work, and her exploding creativity. Jessica's question "Can we paint today?" and her announcement that she knew what she was going to make

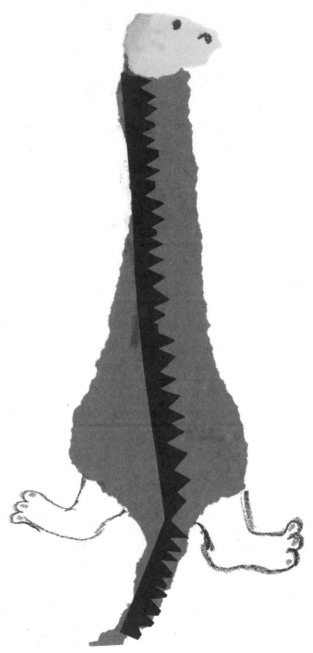

FIGURE 4–8
Jessica's torn-paper dinosaur.

PICTURING LEARNING

made me aware that students were planning ahead, ready to work on their own projects. This convinced me to open the workshop to more choice. Though I had no intention of letting my students paint that day, Jessica pushed me with her questions. Her authentic, persistent, and creative ways allowed me to risk saying yes, cautiously.

As I sat at a table with Jessica and three other students, we discussed their writing. Sandy mentioned that art gave her ideas for writing. Jessica echoed, "Me too—with poems." She looked through her portfolio for an example, saying: "I once was drawing animals. I drew an elephant. Right now I am writing a story called 'Snake Boy.' Drawing animals gave me ideas. I have a lot of animal stories." Jessica went on, "This year I can write better poems. In third grade I'd write silly poems." I questioned her further about how what we had done in art had affected her work in writers workshop, and she responded, "If my story doesn't have pictures in it I don't like it. If I write a poem and then make a picture I like it. Today I'll probably draw a picture, then write about it."

My conversation with Jessica continued after Sandy and the rest of the class left. We sat face to face at the table, and I came back to what she had written earlier that day, questioning her about what she meant by my helping her to "see what I really am." Jessica responded, "You let our imagination wander. We could do anything we wanted," quickly adding, "We couldn't do comics—silly stuff." Jessica described her own surprise at some of her pictures, "the car thing going up the hill, the animal trains, and—" glancing back at her picture (see Plate 9) mounted on a board leaning up against the wall of the classroom gallery, "'Picture of Wonders.' . . . I wasn't really thinking when I put the words on the paper—they just appeared . . . in my mind and I made a poem."

Jessica, like so many of my other students, clearly remembered her process. "With 'Picture of Wonders,' I picked a picture for the poem." She noted that this was the

first time she had ever done the writing and the picture separately.

Our interview had begun as a conversation, and even though I had a line of questioning in mind, that line seemed to take a meandering course, just as the line in my own drawings. We sat in the empty classroom, the stools pushed under the work tables, the signs and banners silently moving in the breeze coming from the open outside door. Jessica quietly offered, "There is something else." Her eyes focused hard in the distance at the redhouse banner hanging in the sharing area. She began to read aloud the passage from Picasso: "'Every child is an artist.' . . . I've always wanted to be an artist—I could look back and tell my child or something that once I wanted to be an artist . . . and it never came true. That poem does mean something, though. Did you want to be an artist when you were a kid?"

"Since I was five," I responded, noting that as easily as my conversation with Jessica and Sandy had led to an informal interview, Jessica had now become the questioner. She offered, "When I was little I had this pad—I'd ask my Dad to draw something and I'd try to draw. . . . I don't know how I got as good at art. . . . My mom's an artist. When I was two I was good at drawing. My favorite artists are van Gogh and Georgia O'Keeffe. I hope I'm an artist . . . not a famous one . . . it makes me happy." She said she did feel like an artist now in contrast to last year when "everything we did was controlled."

She continued to take the lead, wondering about becoming famous, prompting me to describe how, when younger, I had wanted to be famous. She seemed to be piecing together what she had observed about me, how that related to her, while opening up so many new ideas: "I'd like to be a teacher . . . even. . . . It was probably your dream to be famous—you became a teacher. I guess it'd be better to be a teacher. You could help people with their problems. . . . It's funny, I'm only like this in art." In making a comparison to the way she was in other subjects, she described how she felt about art: "I feel like I can do anything. I feel good."

Jessica had brought up the clear memory of what art had meant to me in my life, and without hesitation I offered my fourth-grade questioner an idea I had held since childhood: "When I was growing up I always felt that if everything were taken away from me no one could ever take my art . . . my artistic ability."

Jessica interpreted what I meant in clearer terms: "You could always take a stick and turn it into something. Nobody can ever take your imagination."

I asked her what imagination was and she responded, "It's yourself" and "Everybody does have it—yes. But to feel it, you have to use it." She added that the year before "my pictures were the same as everybody else's."

Jessica shared some of the wonder art had for her and raised some of the issues I had examined throughout the year: how making pictures nudged her into her writing; the importance of choice in her emerging work as an artist and learner; the importance of imagination in learning, in self-expression, and in knowing. In discussing her own work Jessica had to describe the shadows and memories of her parents and artists whom she admired. Apprenticeship, both in the classroom and at a distance, was significant in her learning.

Jessica also told me about my role in this workshop, one where I was questioner, listener, observer, and co-learner. She became the interviewer, pulling out my own thoughts on my apprenticeship and how the arts were significant for me as a way of making meaning. In this interview, one of my students had gone inside the pictures I had been creating throughout the year and rekindled the memories that had helped build this classroom.

Moving Inside   Observing my students, drawing them in my research journal, sitting next to them, asking them questions, often led me to move inside the pictures I was forming of this workshop. I had begun the workshop with a vision that included a framework for a routine based on my beliefs as a practitioner. The role of observer helped me learn what I could do only when I moved inside and listened to the solutions my students were inventing as they faced problems in their work. I continued to question their intentions as they moved forward in their emerging literacy. My students helped me go beyond my vision and brought me solutions to problems I had not even considered.

With my own research journal constantly in hand, I pictured my students as they worked, learning about their projects, intentions, and inquiries. When I sat next to Jerry, a kindergartner, to ask him about the "eyes" he continued to draw, I learned they were not eyes but wheels of "Big Foot, a monster." He then opened his portfolio to show me versions of the monster he had made over the entire year (one is shown in Figure 4–9). He described every picture in his portfolio, even one that had been given to him by a classmate. His picture of a castle reminded me of watching Jerry hard at work, taping pieces of paper together to make the castle bigger each week.

Another time, Emma's asking whether she could "have my portfolio to finish a picture I started last time" reminded me that my students, even the younger ones, were coming to the workshop with their own projects and making connections from one art session to the next. I observed how many students combined their writing and their pictures as they looked forward to the next "poetry reading," when they exhibited their work in the all-school musical performances. Their eagerness to participate in the poetry readings and the all-school hallway art exhibits taught me about the power of ongoing exhibition consciousness. As Portia, a fourth grader, drew line drawings of tumblers for the music program, she would spin around, cross her legs, look down, and return to drawing. She taught me to look for other students using movement as a way into their drawing. As Anthony and Simon coached Carl on how to make brown for the tree in his picture, I

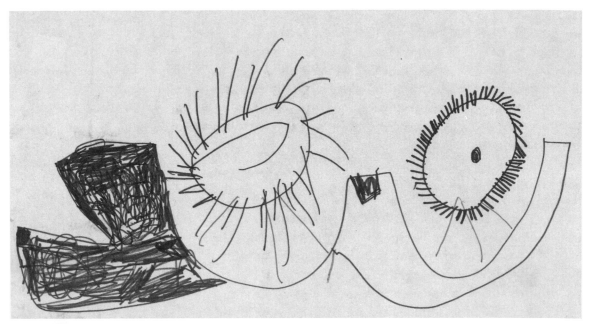

FIGURE 4–9
One of Jerry's "Big Foot" drawings.

learned more about how the work in the art room was collaborative and how students were invested in one another's work. During the concert as Lucy stood at the microphone and showed her picture of a blue pond with a pink horizon, I remembered how one day in art she had described her imagination as "beyond the horizon." Her picture (see Plate 12) was inspired by the impressionists; my questioning had inspired her poem:

> *Imagination*
>
> The green grass
> The blue pond
> The red, yellow, blue flowers
> The pink horizon
> They're all one color
> It's all one imagination
> It's my imagination.

My students' art making had stirred my own imagination. Their writing had let me inside their pictures, and their pictures had led them into their imagination. There were layers of meaning emerging as a result of observation and questioning. My conversation with Jessica when we both questioned and learned from each other became a metaphor for what happened in the artists workshop and for what can happen in any workshop of learning that has observation at its heart. Students become empowered by the knowledge that they make meaning; they take charge of their work and can see and know the world as part of their work. They perceive the teacher as a colleague, as one who is also striving to be an artist, to learn, and to know more.

5

The Expanding Workshop

While setting up my classroom at the beginning of my first year as an art teacher, I had a visitor. Jen bounded down the steps into the art room, appraised the signs dangling overhead, the pots of paint on the table, the almost-ready arrangement of tables and stools, and exclaimed, "This is it!" Jen, now in high school, had been in my eighth-grade class years before and, when she discovered that the arts and aesthetic education were integrated there, had questioned, "Why do we dance in English class?" But now this new room, this artists workshop, appeared familiar to Jen. The memory of Jen and her classmates had helped me envision it, create it, and would help me learn within it. As she described her work in writing at the high school and her involvement in a summer art program, it occurred to me that the real work of the classroom is about how learning moves students and teacher beyond the classroom to other learning, how writing, creating a community, and experiencing the arts empower the students and the teacher. That ownership leads students out and back. There was little talk that day of "do you remember when"; instead, Jen and I discussed our continuing work. I realized that Jen, Linda, Geoff, and others were part of my ongoing work.

FIGURE 5–1
Jenna's geranium drawing showing a classmate in the background.

Now, one of my art classes was sketching a geranium. The small, potted plant sat in the middle of the circle, and the eyes of my students were focused on the green leaves and the red, drooping blossoms. The students were involved in this drawing exercise as a way of seeing. I knew this was a way to open their minds to new possibilities and to have them rehearse for upcoming projects, rather than a way to control them and their time. Earlier in the year, when we had drawn from a stuffed animal model, I felt uneasy about letting students move from that activity to a choice-centered classroom. This was different. My learning had expanded because of my students; their work had stretched the artists workshop beyond my vision. I began to wonder how the workshop affected their learning outside the classroom.

Their intense looking led to simple, clear drawings of a flower, while their writing pointed out that drawing led to close observation. They noticed "it is complicated" and "how the buds grow down" and "the texture of the flower, the various colors." Jenna drew the geranium with a classmate in the background (see Figure 5–1), the use of perspective evident, as she proclaimed, "This is the second sketch I've done in my life." Students took pride in their accomplishments, shared them with others, and recognized their own growth. From my students' writing, I realized the ongoing influence artists had on the students' thinking and their work. One student commented, "I thought about a Georgia O'Keeffe version of the geranium."

Drawing provided a way for the students to notice and record details, this picturing inspired reflective writing, which in turn revealed the students' process. "I felt as if I were climbing and drawing what I climbed," wrote Cathy. Students' writing informed me of the constant influence— and success —that an awareness of the arts provided. Drawing a geranium, painting a landscape, or making an animal collage seemed to be a rehearsal for further learning, theirs and mine, beyond the classroom experience. My intense looking and writing as a participant-observer led to more questions, to pictures of the students' learning beyond the artists workshop.

The elements of writing, art, literature, choice and ownership, authenticity, collaboration and response, exhibition, and apprenticeship, so integral to the workshop, also came into play in students' experiences beyond the classroom. The conversations and writing of students began to show these elements at work as they went outside to make pictures, wrote about how the arts influenced them, visited an art museum, and reviewed their portfolios with their parents.

Going Outside: A New Experience

Lucy perched on the rock at the side of the building, sketching the red barn in the distance. Becky lay on her stomach, drawing the tulips at eye level. As I drew Becky lying face to face with the tulips, another student, also in a prone position, got up to show me her picture of the American flag, which she had drawn from a new perspective. Christina and Maria brought watercolors from the art room and spread them across the sidewalk. Jay announced, "I can't think of anything to draw," then began drawing the crayons and markers lined up on the curb. Students made choices about what to draw and the media they would use, and they seemed to have no trouble selecting from the wide world before them. One student commented, "There are so many things to draw!" Another proudly announced, "I am not drawing something outside," indicating his awareness that imagination always figures in one's choices. The influence of other artists was present. As I observed Matt drawing my former middle school across the playing fields, Jerry remarked, "It looks like one of those Picasso pictures, you know the way he paints them?" In writing about the experience of going outdoors one student stated, "I got my idea from Claude Monet." This variety provided the landscape of our artists workshop as we took our materials, projects, and learning outside.

Carl began his drawing of the tree, while Lawrence captured the delicate quality of tulips and daffodils against the bark of another tree (see Figure 5–2) and Dennis did a delicate marker drawing of the little crab apple tree. When we went outside, students were able to make their selection and focus on the details of what they saw. They wrote about their experience in detail: "You have to look, really look. I was going to draw the flagpole and I didn't think it would be exciting. When I drew it it became exciting."

Another student noted, "When we were outside last week it gave me a feeling to open up my art and to make it look real."

"I learned that I could look at something and draw it from another angle," someone else recorded. "Things looked different as we made the outdoors part of our workshop: I noticed everything looked brighter and more awake when I was ready to draw it than when I just looked at it."

Eileen experienced the outdoors in a different way than ever before: "Warmth, drawing, beginning somewhere that nobody has gone before, looking at flowers differently, so differently that it was like being in space."

I took the younger students outside for their workshop and as I drew them, I listened to their conversations. I realized how I looked forward to new experiences with them instead of shying away as I had earlier in the year. They were silent as they spread across the yard in front of the school; the only sound was the whiz of cars in the background. Patrick remarked about his drawing of the front of the school (see Figure 5–3), "My masterpiece is going along good." Walter leaned over a flower while Nina sat cross-legged, wrapped in the layers and folds of her white smock as she sat concentrating on a daffodil. Kirk tried to climb a tree, but no one was distracted by his antics except me! Kenny told me, "I am drawing two fire monsters fighting with trees . . . in the forest." In our rehearsal we had discussed how artists look at real things in order to make their imaginary pictures appear more real. Kirk, a kindergartner,

FIGURE 5–2
Lawrence's drawing of tulips and daffodils.

PICTURING LEARNING

FIGURE 5–3
Patrick's drawing of the school.

presented me with his drawing: "Miss Ernst sitting under a tree drawing a picture." The older students seemed to focus on detail, while the younger ones were open to the whole world of the real and the imagined.

There was a sincerity in the students as they approached their work; they constantly pushed their own margins of ability and found satisfaction in their pursuit of learning, looking, and creating. When students were empowered to seek their own levels of learning, to engage in their own inquiry, whether drawing a tree or looking at daffodils, there seemed to be an explosion of learning, a performance of skills beyond those that could be charted on paper through tests or other forms of measurement. Sandy had her own goals and outcomes as she went outside. She wrote, "It wasn't a new experience but it felt new, that way it was different. I've never tried as hard in becoming an artist. But when we went outside I tried hard, hard like an artist, and it helped." She went on to describe how art had helped her beyond the art room, "in some spots like writing." Howard Gardner writes, "The assessment of learning also assumes a variety of forms, ranging from the student's monitoring her own learning by keeping a journal to the test of the 'street'" (p. 201). The assessment of learning inside the workshop could only be made accurately once students experienced and described how their learning continued beyond the classroom.

Going Beyond: The Equator, Writing, Everything

There was so much I did not see, could not capture, as my pen wound around the outline of my students when they wrote and drew or were sprawled across the grass in the school yard. My observations and learning always led to more questions. I asked my students, How has the work here in the artists workshop influenced you in other ways, in other classes, or at home? Just as my own choice of drawings and writing surprised me, the words of my young informants surprised me as well. Nicole philosophically described how imagination had become real to her: "Well, in art I've learned to use my imagination more. For example, when I was little I didn't believe people when they said the equator was invisible, and now I do." Another student took the idea of collaboration home to help his younger brother approach making pictures in a new way: "It is amazing how one little speck of a different color can make such a big difference. My artwork and art experiences help me out in school and at home. For example, at home my brother was painting a picture; it looked very dull, so I taught him how to make a splatter paint. My brother thought it was too messy, so he came up with a big dot picture and that made his picture look a lot better."

Students described how their work in the art room helped them "make maps better" and frequently linked their work to writing. "Art has given me a good influence on writing by learning how to use my imagination much better." "I've become a better writer, and that writing goes to my pictures.... I've learned how to look at pictures more closely and [get] the feeling of that picture." They described how the workshop had helped in other subjects as well: "It helped me in piano class because I thought drawing is like making music, so if I could draw I could play it."

James provided my biggest revelation. New to the school, he came to art with great enthusiasm as he leaned over his paper each week, worked intensely, and seemed to find joy in what he did. I was always puzzled because his pictures (see the one shown in Figure 5–4, for example) seemed filled with scribbles and color, and to my eyes lacked a focus. One day James wrote in his artists notebook (see Figure 5–5), "Art has inspired me to look at the earth closer, to see its pure color. Like the beautiful reflection of a sunset on a beach, like paint spilled in water. At school it inspires me to write. Art is everything." James's accomplishments were not evident as I looked at his pictures. But his work in the artists workshop was helping him notice detail, write vividly, and express himself through writing and poetry.

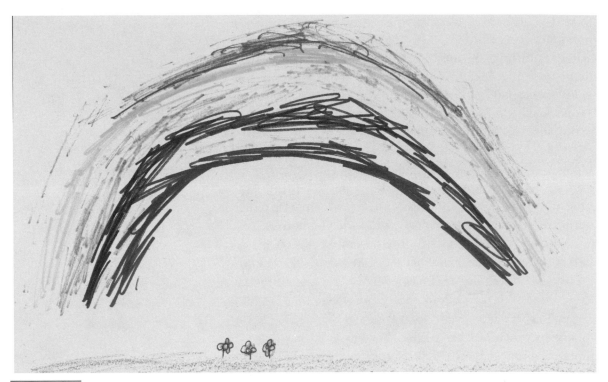

FIGURE 5–4
One of James's pictures.

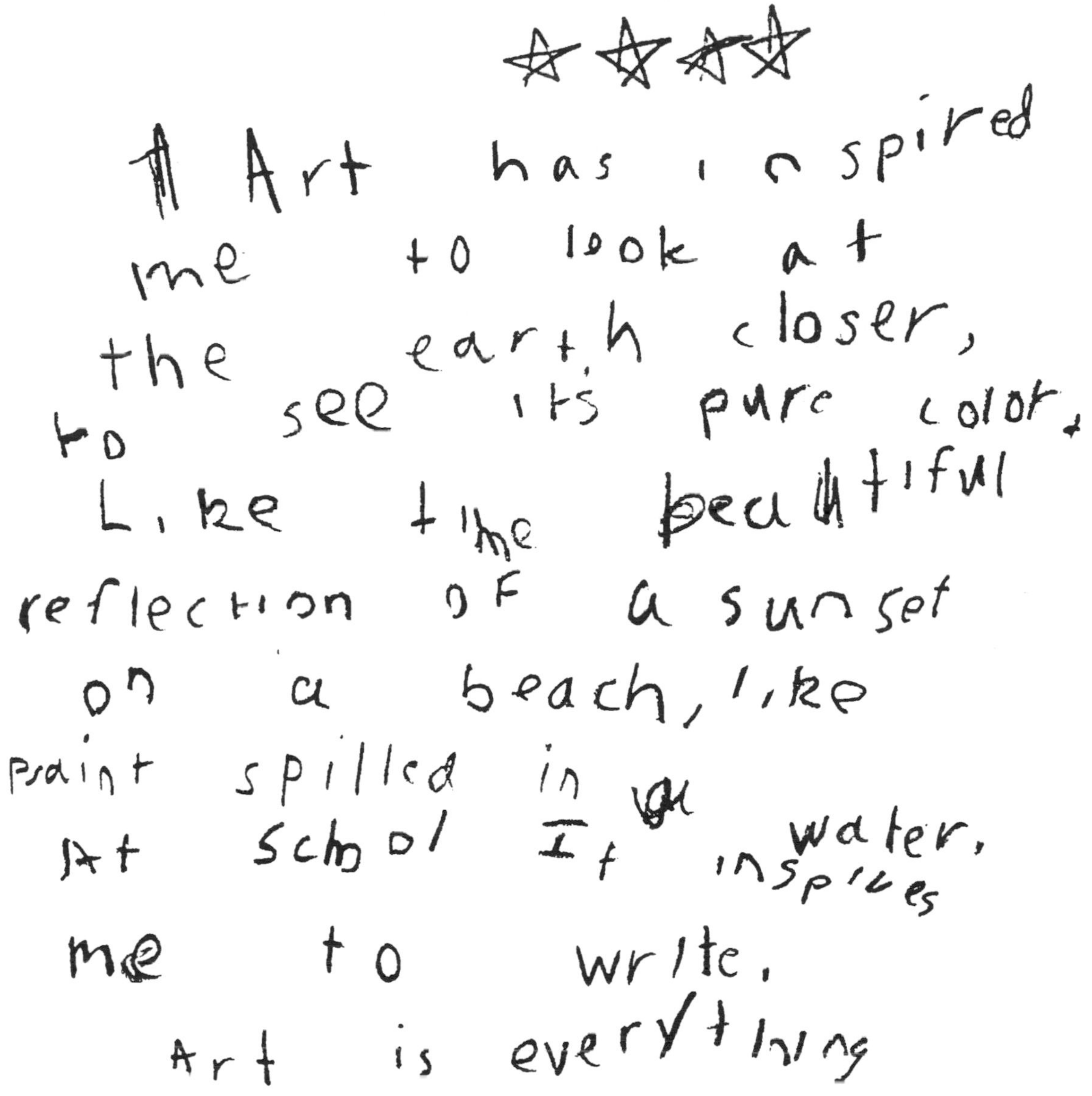

☆☆☆☆

¶ Art has inspired
me to look at
the earth closer,
to see its pure color,
Like the beautiful
reflection of a sunset
on a beach, like
paint spilled in a
At school It water,
inspires
me to write.
Art is everything

FIGURE 5–5
A page from James's notebook.

Maxine Greene (1978) writes that "if involvement with the arts and humanities has the potential for provoking precisely this sort of reflectiveness, we need to devise ways of integrating them into what we teach at all levels of the educational enterprise" (p. 163). My students were teaching me the ways they were taking their learning beyond the classroom, owning their experiences, taking it to "the test of the street."

Looking for Monet, Finding Picasso, and More

"I am looking for the Monet," one boy remarked as he passed his classmates, who were sprawled on the floor of the museum, concentrating, writing about, and sketching the original works in the galleries of the Wadsworth Atheneum in Hartford, Connecticut. As I moved from one gallery to the next on the museum's three floors, I drew groups of students talking as they huddled around a painting. Everyone I passed seemed to ask, "Where is 'The Sunbather'?"

In preparing for the two visits, one with the entire third grade, another with one fourth-grade class, I had shown slides of fifteen works at the museum. "The Sunbather," a sculpture by Duane Hanson, was memorable because "it looked like a real person." (A student's sketch of "The Sunbather" is shown in Figure 5–6.) The slides I used represented the broad range of styles the students would see at the museum. Each subgroup, led by a parent, was on its own as the students viewed the artwork as well as the Gothic architecture and outdoor sculpture of the oldest public art museum in the United States.

While viewing the slides the students demonstrated their ability to discuss the work, telling what they saw and felt, what story came to mind, and the technique of the artist. One boy commented that he recognized a painting by Renoir as "just like the book you read us about a painter." He saw a similarity between "Monet Painting in His Garden" and Gregory in Cynthia Rylant's *All I See*. From the early preparation through the day of the trip I

FIGURE 5–6
A student rendition of "The Sunbather."

observed the students, read their writing and pictures, and listened to their discussions; I saw their ability to identify and make connections with literature, art, and the works of other students as well as their own.

Although the initial focus of the students was a search for paintings by Monet and for other favorite works, for the most part this was a day of looking, learning, responding to the works of artists, and rediscovering some that had influenced their work during the year: "Miss Ernst, we saw Georgia O'Keeffe!" Through the trip to the museum, students were going beyond looking at works simply to determine whether they liked them. They became involved with works of art through their own drawing and writing. It was a day of expanding the learning in the artists workshop. Vincent's voice resounded in the quiet of the museum: "Picasso is in here!"

When we arrived, the students and the parents wound their way around the castlelike museum. Then they looked up at the kinetic sculptures by Calder and approached the enormous red door. As the guard icily opened the door to the museum and the young students entered, they recognized Eric Segal's "The Trapeze Artist" hanging overhead in the lobby. It seemed to welcome them.

They checked their backpacks and lunch bags, and Kelly cautioned me, "You better watch these moms, Miss Ernst!" Her experience in the workshop prepared her to recognize that this was a personal experience; she had her own project but worried that the parents would act as guides, telling the students what to look for or leading the discussion. Kelly and the others wanted this to be a collaborative effort. They were driven by their choice of artwork, they had an opportunity to respond through discussion, and they intended to make their own ideas known through writing and drawing. The students were expected to select at least one work of art to respond to; they were to draw it and write about it. I asked them to capture what it looked like, how it made them feel, what it reminded them of, why they selected it, or what story they saw in the work. I assured Kelly that the parents would know what to do.

Prior to the trip, the teachers and parents who participated had their early morning preparation session. I showed them the same slides I had shown my students and outlined the agenda and expectations for the trip. I familiarized them with the works and asked them to respond and to describe what they saw. This museum trip expanded our community of learners by bringing together the students and their parents.

Pictures of an Exhibition

I walked through the museum hoping to capture the intensity with which these third and fourth graders approached their day at the museum. Students saw paintings that reminded them of other works of art or literature we had discussed during the year. While sketching Milton Avery's "Husband and Wife" (see Figure 5–7), one boy commented, "It reminds me of that book we saw with no faces," remembering Goennel's *Sometimes I Like to Be Alone*. As I passed Renee she told me that "Chambered Nautilus" by Andrew Wyeth reminded her of Burnett's *The Secret Garden*. Neil spent a long time in a gallery drawing a painting "exactly like another painting I saw in another museum." The fact that literature and art were integral parts of the classroom experience pushed the students to make connections between what they saw and what they knew—what they had read or experienced.

As a result of our year-long practice of looking at and discussing art, students knew they could each have a different response as they discussed the artwork at the museum: "I like how they draw the faces and make them look so real," one said; or, as Michael asked Cal, "How many faces do you see in this picture?" Cliff said he wanted to do a sketch of Ernest Lawson Winters's "Spuyten Duyvil" and also of a Jackson Pollack. He liked the way the "paint layered." Heather sketched Robert Arneson's "Head of

FIGURE 5–7
A sketch of Milton Avery's "Husband and Wife."

Jackson Pollack" and wrote, "I saw lots of different things like optical illusions. I saw three shapes in a stripe but I looked up suddenly and it had moved."

In the same room as the much-sought-after "Sunbather" was a freestanding cut-out painting of an elderly woman, "Margie" by Alex Katz. Julie did a sketch from the back; Ellen did one from the front (see Figure 5–8). Two groups of third graders and their parents were seated in silence on the floor sketching beyond "The Sunbather" to their new focus of interest, Wesselman's "The Great American Nude #69" (one of the results is shown in Figure 5–9). Max wrote about the painting, "It reminds me of when I went to Spain and saw a nudist beach. It looks like a cartoon." Jeff's sketch caught the cartoon quality, too, but his accompanying comment showed his delight in experiencing the museum with his mother: "I had a great time because Mom was there." Ginny had still another version of Wesselman, but chose to write of the misfortune that "the Monets were rented" and commented that she "liked searching, it was hard to write, some looked real." Noel drew "The Sunbather" from a different perspective, writing, "When I came to where 'The Sunbather' was I thought from looking far away that it was a real person posing for the picture. I mean I just can't stop talking about that one."

Alicia took my hand and pulled me over to look at Daniel Maclise's "The Disenchantment of Bottom," reminding me of our reading Shakespeare's *A Midsummer Night's Dream* earlier in the year. Even though I had shown the students fifteen slides to prepare them for the trip, they understood that they were not limited to looking at just those works. Certainly the work of artists was part of the workshop rehearsal, but the students' activity in both the workshop and the museum was a matter of their own choice.

Vincent seemed to forget he was away from the artists workshop. After he finally located the Picasso and did a

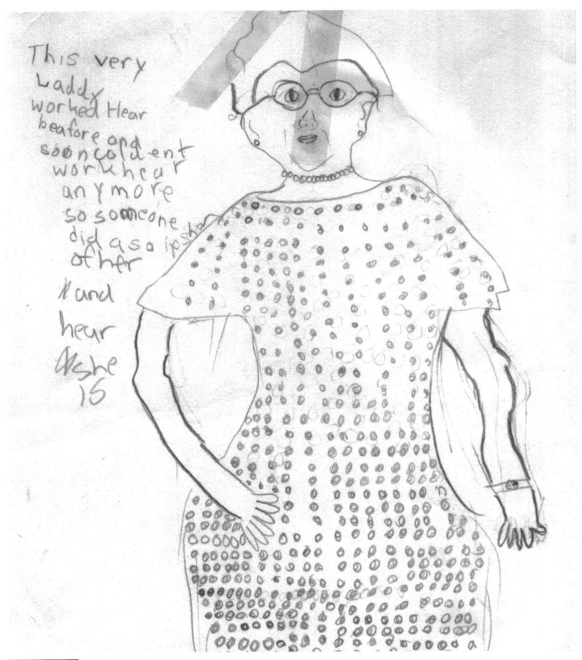

This very
Laddy
worked Hear
beafore and
soon coldent
work hear
anymore
so someone
did a solipsha
other
it and
hear
she
is

FIGURE 5–8
Ellen's version of Alex Katz's "Margie."

the great American Nood

Artist tom Wesselman

FIGURE 5–9
One student's "The Great American Nude #69."

quick sketch, he turned to me excitedly and asked, "Can we paint now?" As groups ate their bag lunches in the Calder Court and ran under and around the gigantic orange metal "Stegosaurus" as if it were recess, I too almost forgot we were away from school. These third and fourth graders seemed to own the museum that day.

The students' written comments ranged from things they noticed about the artwork to their critique of the trip. Amanda's writing was about the "hurt feelings" she experienced, while Kathleen was not too pleased with what she found at the museum: "Only a few paintings interested me. So I only sketched one. Alicia wrote, "I loved 'The Sunbather,' but unfortunately I could not draw her. . . . My favorite was the 'Praying Mantis.' But it was hard to concentrate because of my tooth." Students used writing to communicate their thoughts and approached the museum as learners, artists, and children. As I sketched Claire and Renee drawing Bloom's "The Italian Straw Hat" and Margie drawing Barth's "The Negro Looks Ahead," I knew that their sketches and my drawings of them helped us see, think about, and understand our experiences that day.

I observed a seriousness, a focus, and a personal learning on the part of the students and the parents, both. James was sitting under a huge Josef Kline painting. "Why do you like this one?" I asked. He continued sketching while he responded, "It's not hard. It's not plain, kind of like reminds me of Westport. It reminds me of the minuteman statue for a strange reason. It's different." Carl was in the Milton Avery room doing a drawing of Albreight's "I Slept with the Starlight in My Face." He said, "This kind of showed me how to sketch or paint 3D." Artists' works continued to provide students with distant apprenticeships, helping them learn new techniques at their own pace.

Sondra was huddled next to her mom as she drew Georgia O'Keeffe's "The Lawrence Tree." Her mother commented, "Thank you so much for getting me into a museum.

It's been too long." This experience at the museum gave the parents an opportunity to make their own observations about the process of learning in the artists workshop and then write about them through a series of questions I sent home. They commented on the museum, the preparation for the trip, the attention of the students, the works of art, and the trip as a learning experience, and they offered suggestions about how we might improve future trips.

Most parents felt the orientation meetings were helpful and noted that the students were clear in their purpose at the museum. This allowed the parents to feel more comfortable and enabled them to let the children discuss, draw, and write. "With my group there was no prodding to get into the assignment; the children just seemed to flow with it. The slides seemed to give them a focus but did not get in the way of enjoying unfamiliar artwork." Another parent noticed the students' focus. "The group decided on their own what they wanted to draw and were quite serious about doing this. I particularly liked watching my son lying down in a museum sketching and writing." One parent who had missed the orientation said she "felt like a taskmaster, frustrated with my own child. My expectations and wishes got in the way of my experience." These comments reminded me of the importance of rehearsal, of stepping back to let students discover and express meaning.

In this experience at the museum, where the parents were able to observe and interact with the students, the children provided apprenticeships for the parents by modeling how to engage with works of art and with one another. Parents offered their observations of the serious involvement they witnessed. One recalled "Sondra and her mother telling about what the dark blob was in the O'Keeffe painting." Another wrote, "I was amazed that such a static painting got him so involved in a story." One parent noted: "I really like to sketch. I was surprised at my results and how much the sketch freed my mind to write poems about the painting rather than break them down or analyze them." Another parent wrote, "There were three teenagers watching the boys sketch, and one commented that he wished he had done that when he was younger." Gardner recommends that schools be more like museums, where students observe, interact, and experience apprenticeships with a number of adults. Through our museum trip, the older visitors and parents had apprenticeships with children!

Taking Responsibility for Learning

These third and fourth graders had assumed responsibility for their learning before they arrived at the huge red door of the museum; they came prepared to look, draw, write, and respond in their own way to the artwork. Just as students in writers workshop read as writers, these students went as artists and learners looking at art. They responded to this experience after the visit: "I don't always have to draw something real" or "You have to think before you draw." They related the work in the museum to their own: "Well, some of their paintings were like mine, like I do designs and lots of them do too." They acquired new ideas in their apprenticeships with artists: "I got ideas to make things that I see in my own way." They wrote about "learning to look at art" and "finding its value to you" and "looking hard." "Using our imagination" helped prepare them for this experience. They were ready and they were looking for Monet, Picasso, or O'Keeffe, as well as new techniques to add to their own artistic repertoire. One parent wrote: "It seems to me that you've not taught them art but how to learn about art. Having learned how to learn makes them so much stronger as people. It was special to be a learner with the children." A student wrote, "We have learned how to appreciate art, how to read the story it tells." Another suggested, "We learned that everybody is different in their way of thinking and their way of words."

Following the trip, one fourth grader used her regular classroom journal to respond to fourteen paintings she remembered. She referred to both literature and personal experience: "'Moonrise' by Ralph Albert Blakelock . . . reminds me of the blue lagoon in 'The Little Mermaid.' 'The Nooning' by Winslow Homer [makes me think] of St. Joe, Michigan, on the first day of summer at my grandpa's house; 'Winter Scene Rameo Valley' by Jasper Francis Craskey—of a Christmas picture." She ended her journal entry with: "I remember when we went to the Wadsworth Atheneum. We taught [Miss Ernst] what we had learned."

Just as a museum holds the potential for teaching and stimulating learning, workshops of learning in schools can be like museums and more. Students can learn to take charge of their learning, so that when they go beyond the classroom to museums, to concerts, to libraries, when they meet with adults or experts in a discipline, they can model and become apprentices. They can continue to learn, question, and respond.

Portfolio Review: Inside Pictures and Learning

Mom kept every picture in a box. . . . Some pictures were drawn with crayons or pencil; others were painted in watercolor. I spent summers drawing, alone or with a friend, looking outside my window, at books, or into my imagination. I have that special box of pictures, the paper now yellowed by over thirty years. It holds pictures of Mickey Mouse, drawings of the crab apple tree in the front yard, dogs, and little girls from coloring and comic books. That box still makes me feel special because it reminds me that my mom thought my drawings and I were special. Within that box was my lifelong desire to be an artist.

First grader Alice made her portfolio review a real family affair. "I showed it to my grandparents, and they liked it and their favorite was the leopard; the second favorite was the one of Gerald. I shared it with my parents, and we liked the overlapping one. I shared with my whole family, and they liked all of my pictures. My mom and dad liked the one where I drew a picture of my sister under the rainbow." Claire, a second grader, described how her brother

Carl, a kindergartner, brought his portfolio home and shared it with the entire family as well, and offered that she liked his "Indian design" and his "Ninja turtle." Watching a group of students board the bus with portfolios in hand heightened the anticipation for other students as they waited their turn to share their pictures and stories with their parents and families in what we called portfolio reviews. Through these conversations about the work in artists workshop, parents got an opportunity to track the progress of their children's work while looking at and discussing it with them. Students like Alice and Claire had a chance to share more than just pictures with their entire family. Arranging this review just prior to parent conferences provided an opportunity to include the child's work in art as part of the conversation about the child's entire picture of learning.

Portfolios went home and were returned in two days with a review. The arts became a topic of conversation about learning both in the workshop and in the hallways. As a parent passed me in the hallway, she said: "I went over my son's portfolio and I wrote it all down." She laughed and added, "He said he loves art but he said, 'The art teacher makes me think too hard.'" Another parent learned in her fourth grader's conference that "my daughter approaches her writing through her art." "I've gotten better," one kindergartner said. A second grader related, "First we looked through all of my paintings and my mom said 'What do you think?' . . . She's going to frame all of them, I think." Portfolios taught the parents about the process and progress of their child's work in the artists workshop.

Just as evaluation conferences were part of my eighth grade writers workshop, these portfolio reviews provided me with new information about my students' learning. The portfolios, collections of writing or pictures, were the most reliable basis I had for individual evaluation. In writers workshop I had not graded individual pieces of writing

Instead, using Atwell's model, I met with each student in an evaluation conference. We reviewed the student's work for the quarter, we discussed priorities for learning, we set goals for the next quarter, and we agreed on a grade for reading and writing. During that important week, my other roles were put on hold. I sat at the table conferring with one student at a time in the silence of my classroom, while the others read, wrote, and prepared for their own conferences. They had an opportunity to review their own work, reflect on and establish their own goals, and inform me of breakthroughs in learning that I would not have been able to ascertain otherwise. The conference led to increased ownership in learning for the students and, for me, a deeper understanding of my students and their work. These conferences were the most valuable learning experiences I had in my own classroom. I came to the artists workshop with a firm belief in the value of keeping portfolios, and my experience validated the importance of reviewing the portfolio in the process of evaluation.

In order to have a conference with each of my 365 students, I decided to engage the help of the parents by sending home the portfolio and a letter describing how to conduct a conference. It included questions to guide the conversation (see Figure 5–10). As in writers workshop, the quarterly evaluation conference began as an interview. By including parents in this interview process, I hoped to expand their learning as well as my own. The response was gratifying: 98 percent of the portfolios were returned with parent comments recording the conversations they'd had with their children. Through this process I gained information about students' ideas and inspirations. Through it, I was assured that the components of a workshop of learning were present. Students were planning ahead, choosing from a wide range of sources, and progressing toward ownership and self-evaluation. Pride in student work, students' ability to identify new skills and attitudes, and the important role of imagination were emphasized in review after review. Many students asked for more time in art.

Portfolio Review

Dear Parents of _____,

This is your child's portfolio in art which he/she has been keeping since September. I would like your help in doing a "Portfolio Review" with your child by looking through the work with him/her and asking the questions I have listed below. This will give you a chance to see his/her work, talk with him/her about it, and give me more information on his/her progress. Of course I will share this with the classroom teacher.

Use the questions as a guide, noting responses and any other comments resulting from your conversations. Return the Portfolio and Portfolio Review in the bag provided in two days.

Thank you for you help and I hope you enjoy the "Portfolio Review."

Sincerely,
Karen Ernst, Art Teacher

The Questions

1. Tell me about some of the pictures. What are they about? How did you make them?

2. What picture(s) do you like best? Why?

3. Where did you get your ideas?

4. How do you think you have changed as an artist since September? How has your work changed?

5. Is there anything about your work that you would like to say?

FIGURE 5–10
Letter to parents and questions for students.

Pictures Are Stories

"I love the picture of the vase with flowers, sitting on the pretty tablecloth. I really love the way I did the tablecloth. It was hard to do, but I think it came out good." Students proudly discussed their best works; most students described three or four, but many kindergartners described ten or more, detailing the story behind each picture, ranking it in order of how they perceived its quality. Keith, a kindergartner, discussed seventeen of the pictures in his portfolio, including "my imagination painting with footprints of ducks, a Georgia O'Keeffe flower, Ninja, army team, Little Mermaid, a horse, a painting of feelings." Often the "best" was selected, showing the student's ability to discuss a new skill or technique: "The one with the rainbow. I like the way the clouds are painted in white with blue so they really look like clouds. I painted the colors right next to each other so it really looks like a rainbow. The flowers are little dots like they are in the bushes."

Ideas for pictures were inspired by interests: fire trucks, rainbows, flowers, Ninja turtles, castles, books they had read, experiences they had had: "I get my ideas from books I read, from my friends and from events I attend. Grandpa inspired the Indian picture." Others said they were inspired by artists and friends: "I get most of my ideas from the books I read and also the books I write. I get some ideas from paintings and from friends."

"I just found them in my head. Sometimes it's my house, sometimes it's the sky and rainbows, and sometimes it's from stories like Noah's ark or the little Indian boy" (dePaola's *The Legend of the Indian Paintbrush*). Kevin described how the role of imagination was essential to his work, and he seemed proud to own the ability to come up with ideas. Imagination, often described as part of the head, was an important element of inspiration for students. Lawrence's use of imagination led to a new confidence in expressing his feelings. His mother wrote, "Lawrence likes the lion [see Figure 5–11], the mountains, his drawing with writing in it." Lawrence told his mom, "Two come directly

FIGURE 5–11
Lawrence's lion.

from my mind, and the third is a sketch of an object from the art room. By expressing my feelings directly from my imagination I am more confident in letting out my feelings. Drawing a picture or painting is not a way of saying I'm a good artist. It is a way of expressing my imagination and feelings." Rita's work in art was also a form of expression: "I go into my pictures. When I draw a picture I say, 'Where will I go?'" These students illustrate the belief that the arts play a crucial role in enhancing the ability to think, imagine, and express ideas in both pictures and words.

In describing five favorites Marissa explained, "These are the ones I learned myself. It was from my imagination; the others I learned from other people, like Samantha. I didn't copy. I took my imagination and I looked in my mind and it was like I drew my mind." She explained, "Samantha is so good, she's like my teacher, but she doesn't know it."

Students were influenced by the literate community of the workshop where literature was essential to the rehearsal and where collaboration was integral to the ongoing work. Some of Leslie's ideas came "from *Mouse Paint* [Walsh] . . . from a rainbow, and artwork that was on the walls, and one idea I got from Shelly." Simon got his ideas from books like *The Lion, the Witch, and the Wardrobe* (C. S. Lewis), and from artists: "The house in the meadow [was] inspired by a painting by van Gogh." The outdoors inspired him as well: "The colors of the seasons, each tree symbolizing a season and the dominating color." His mother wrote, "He says he has improved in making shadows, using colors, he's better at sketching from real life." Students were able to evaluate their own work seriously and authentically, showing how they were engaged in this process and indicating their ownership in the challenge of learning.

Kevin's favorite was "the Gallery ship [see Figure 3–11 on page 80]; it was in Magellan's or Columbus's fleet." He "liked the shapes, and it looks like it was sketched by a real artist." His ideas came "either from my imagination or from talking with a friend or from looking at a famous painting." Students continuously expressed the concept of imagination as a place from which ideas come. The classroom environment, which included the work of artists, was essential to inspiring students in their work. Choice within the workshop encouraged a wide range of ideas while the responses in the reviews showed the variety of sources for ideas. Karen described the importance of choice in the workshop: "It's changed a lot. Last year we couldn't choose. We didn't get to do our own ideas. Now I get to take my ideas out of my head."

In describing their change over the months in artists workshop students told of their ability to use detail: "I draw people with more detail, I didn't draw noses before." They described an increased understanding of technique, using colors, making shadows, sketching from real life: "[I have the] ability to draw realistically" or "I used to draw designs, now I am more realistic." They spoke about an increase in their confidence: "I can draw more things now, and I'm not afraid to try anymore." Many students expressed their ability to think ahead or plan ahead: "I think a lot. I wait and I think and I just paint the picture after I thought it" or "I draw pictures with a bigger scene and now I form a picture in my head and I put it on paper. I didn't do that in September." Frank, a second grader, indicated his pride in changing as an artist and taking ownership of the work in his portfolio: "Before I do art, I think about it really hard, and then I put my feelings down on paper. I usually like doing abstracts with squiggly lines. . . . I get my ideas from the feeling of the day. . . like if it's a hot day I draw people with short sleeves. I like to relax and have a good time when I paint my abstracts—it's just amazing how I get it to look so good. I've changed a lot. What I used to do as an artist was I used to have a lot of mess-ups. Now I just use the mess-ups to make my picture better. What else? I love it! Nobody tells me how to do art."

When students make their own choices for projects, they are in charge of their learning and progress and they increase their skills and attitudes at their own pace and with great enthusiasm. George responded, "There is more movement in my pictures now. I look at my pictures different. I let my pencil run with my mind, which makes movement." Students demonstrated their ability to attend to detail in their work, described the steps of their progress, and indicated a new ability to look, to observe, to notice. Spanish-speaking kindergartner Theresa and her mother were able to articulate a learning that for me went beyond the expected idea of technique or speculation about where ideas come from. Theresa's work in the artists workshop was helping her to notice the world: "I feel great because before I ignore this world. . . . I feel great because I so happy of start to learn this new language and also understand the things I saw in the whole world. Thank you."

Students loved finding that they could use their talent to fix mistakes. They realized that making a mistake is not the end of a picture. You can make it a part of the picture. "I like the idea of changing a mistake into a new idea and then you come out with a totally different picture." Experimentation was often mentioned as a way to get ideas: "I just try new things, think of how Jackson [the raccoon in the Glass story] threw around paint," one student said. Another explained, "I get my ideas from other paintings, other people, my mind, and trying new things."

The pictures prompted discussion of the details of the students' work and the stories that were held in the pictures. Providing a workshop environment and a routine that encouraged collaboration, a place rich with literature and art, stimulated their imagination and contributed significantly to the literate community. I realized that children were discovering the profound power of art when they turned mistakes into meaning and when they recognized that they could control the outcome of their pictures.

Portfolios of Learning

The variety of Vinny's work, among others', showed me the importance of keeping all work in the portfolio, since together these pictures held the stories, the history, of a student's work and learning in the artists workshop. Vinny commented, "I made some, copied some, just scribbled on one, some I couldn't finish. . . . In one I was thinking about a river and painted my feelings. . . . One was a sunset copied from a book, but enlarged. One was a flower someone had painted and I made one too. One was abstract mixing colors. My friend drew one, and I tried to draw it after him. . . . I take lots of time doing each paper. If I mess up tons of times 'cause it's hard to do, I'll just keep doing it until it looks right." The evaluation conferences helped me analyze my progress as a teacher and my role in the workshop. The students' responses made me aware of my use of the word "imagination" and my frequent recommendations to turn mistakes into something.

"Leslie was able to explain what every picture was and what they were made of," her mother wrote. Parents gained insight into their children's thinking and expressed their support of a choice-centered classroom. The parent-child review produced information, allowed students to reflect, and informed a wider audience about the ongoing learning in artists workshop. One parent wrote a letter that she enclosed in her daughter's portfolio. "When Sondra brought her portfolio home, I opened it and quickly looked through it. My initial response was, 'Is this all you have done in art this year?'" However, Sondra's mom went on to describe what she had learned after that initial look as she followed the directions in my letter and engaged her daughter in a conversation about the pictures and meanings within the portfolio. The parent-student conversations were an important part of the process of learning in our workshop. The portfolio review, like the work in the artists workshop, was not just concerned with looking at pictures but revealed the multifaceted process of understanding the meaning, the stories, the inspiration, the new attitudes, and the learning held inside the pictures.

"You don't have a story or a picture about me "
(my fear as a researcher).

Now I do

6
To Keep Going

On May 3, 1990, I wrote in my journal, "I remembered what I had written with my students as they responded to the question I posed to them: How has the work here in the artists workshop influenced you in other ways? Teaching art has helped me weave together the strands of my life: writing, drawing, teaching, pretending, imagining, and learning. Teaching art has helped me bring to work my own ability to pretend as a child. I have imagined this room into an artists studio...even to the point where some kids call me the artist. And if what we do has made Nicole believe in the imaginary line of the equator, I think this year has made me believe in myself as an artist and teacher."

As I moved toward the last session of the year with each class, my private project became to write a picture book I called "The Art Teacher," a title I based on Tomie dePaola's *The Art Lesson*. When I had prepared for the first sessions in September, I wondered what I would do next, what minilesson or book I would use, if I would ever know all of the new names and faces. Now I knew their names, faces, and their pictures of learning, and I was looking not for a particular lesson but for an appropriate ending. I was leaving for the same reason I had come: because of decreasing enrollment and low seniority, I was losing my job as a teacher in the district. I was keenly aware that it had taken me twenty-two years, perhaps a lifetime, to become an art teacher. I had never lost sight of the importance of my own experience in kindergarten, of drawing a red house and having my teacher notice it and me, and deciding then to be an artist.

I thought of this story as a gift to my students, a way I could tell them what they had given me, and to show them how my story is a version of theirs. I wanted my story of this workshop to remind them of their knowledge and all they learned through pictures or words. I knew that the memories of my childhood, my quest as an artist, and my work as a teacher were part of the fabric of the classroom. My story was a driving force behind what I did in envisioning this artists workshop.

Anne Haas Dyson writes, "Like children, we, as educators, organize our experiences through stories. We pull together the streams of classroom actions and actors into cohesive events that we imbue with our own attitudes and values, our own perspectives on teaching and learning" (p. 192). Creating the book and identifying the story seemed to help me move toward the ending, to understand what it was that I wanted to happen and what actually did happen here.

When the students entered the art room for their final session, the easel directed: "Meet me on the rug." When they were settled, facing the green chair where I had sat for the last forty weeks, I began to read and show my story. The big, blue-covered book sat opened to the pages written for my students, including drawings of our classroom and of them, and of pictures I had made when I was very young. It was dedicated to my mother. The story began in my classroom but centered on a memory of when I was in kindergarten: "A big, white banner hangs in my classroom. On it is a red house with a blue roof. It is like a picture I made in kindergarten. It was then I knew...I wanted to be an art teacher when I grew up."

As I finished reading to each class the younger students talked about the parts they liked before returning to the tables to work. I asked the third and fourth graders to return to their work tables to write a response to my book or a memory of a time when they felt like an artist. Portia, a fourth grader, wrote, "My memory is that when I was in first grade I drew a picture that felt important to me. But when I brought it home my mom said that it was beautiful. And she kept it on the refrigerator for three years. It was a picture of a pig looking at you behind a fence." Portia let me know how important positive support is, how it can affect us for a lifetime. How can we continue at school what most moms do so well when we are very young?

Lawrence, a fourth grader, wrote, "I think what stood out in Miss Ernst's book was the picture that she drew when she was nine or ten. What really got to me was the picture of the three dogs playing with the jump rope. What I think really made me feel like a real artist was the picture that I drew of a bunch of flowers in a group and a picture that I drew of a flower with a tree behind the flower." Lawrence's memory gave me hope that during this year in artists workshop there were countless discoveries and pictures that allowed the students to feel like accomplished artists or writers. These discoveries might propel their literacy, and they might use pictures as part of that process. As a researcher, knowing that happens is important, but as a teacher, opening the possibility for it to happen is crucial.

Justine, a third grader, wrote, "I felt like an artist once when I went in my grandpa's art studio and he showed me paints and gave me some kind of special crayons and when I sat in his art chair and he showed me his pictures." Apprenticeship has an impact on children's learning and attitudes. Asking students to do what real artists, writers, scientists, and mathematicians do, and modeling our learning endeavors, are part of authentic learning. Students can learn by seeing the work of real artists, by showing their work in class, by reading the stories of master writers, by keeping journals, by learning how to see, by using their imagination.

Allen wrote, "I remember sketching outside. I remember my Superman drawing. My painting with lots of colors was one of my favorites. I remember reciting my poem called 'Rocket Smoke' to the school. My collage with the sailor was different. That's why I liked it. This was my favorite art year. I had a lot of freedom at last." As researchers and teachers, we use our students as informants to help us know what to do next based on what steps they have made toward success, according to their goals. Students chose their own works for the exhibitions, critiqued other students' work, and used what they noticed for their own work. An exhibition consciousness developed, and memories, like Allen's, of showing work in an assembly or on the wall created lasting moments of learning that empowered students to move forward in their work and in their attitude about learning. By attending to that information, students became good art and writing teachers for one another and for me. Listening to their stories about their pictures informed me of their progress, which often I could not see. I had to listen as well.

Choice, what Allen called freedom, was the core of this workshop of learning. When students make their own choices for pictures, projects, stories, or problems to solve, they engage in their work with an enthusiasm and ownership that cannot be matched when work is assigned. They have a stake in the outcome, in their learning, and can move toward becoming creative individuals. Students described "getting to do what you want" as important, but as I learned from Jessica in her interview, it is equally important to provide guidelines. Along with the components of choice and ownership were modeling through minilessons and the inspiration provided through reading literature, showing art, discussing students' work, and having rehearsals for learning. These were the components that brought an authenticity to the learning. But when students take control of their own learning and have their own projects, teachers must decide whether to provide models or give students more time. Knowing that this tension exists helps teachers answer the challenges students face when they are ready to go to work.

In addition to the written responses to my story, I ended the year with other images: Christina, excelling in making pictures, finding meaning in that, letting her picture making push her learning in the difficult areas of math, reading, and writing. Christina's success in the artists workshop was praised; then it was ignored when her placement for the following year was decided. Other ways of finding meaning—making pictures, writing songs, and exploring dance—need to be provided in the classrooms, not just as a means of freeing students but also as a part of their emerging literacy. Students like Christina need opportunities to use their expertise in art to help them become better readers, writers, and thinkers.

Observing and writing about Christina convinced me that the arts are integral to learning, not merely a separate or special subject. When the arts are made an integral part of the curriculum they can be used as "a methodology for acquiring knowledge, as subject matter, and as an array of expressive opportunities" (Gallas, p. 40). When schools move toward integrating subjects, students will have a range of ways to explore ideas, find solutions, and express themselves. This will encourage teachers to collaborate, to share their expertise in disciplines, and to learn from one another.

I understood the impact of my story, "The Art Teacher," through conversations with my students and through their written words. Writing was a form of thinking and expression in the artists workshop. Some students chose to write instead of make pictures; others used writing to express or discover the meaning in their pictures, or to remember ideas of pictures, or to think about, revise, and assess their pictures and process. Here words were partners with pictures, complementing students' processes, propelling their thinking. One student explained the relationship between pictures and words like this: "It's given me ideas. After, I draw my art. You need your brain for both. In art you have to think what your topic will be. In writing you have to think what your story will be." As Nancie Atwell says, writing cannot be left to the English teachers; it must be an essential element in all workshops of learning.

The portfolio reviews reminded me how important it is to encourage students to use their imagination. I was fascinated when they described imagination as part of their bodies or as a separate section of their heads. However imagination was defined by these young students, they indicated that it was connected to an increased self-confidence in their learning, ownership of their projects, and an opening to ideas. Because I emphasized imagination in the workshop, students were able to talk about how colors could describe how they felt. They could go inside a picture to write about what they found or describe the story in their picture.

As learning inside the workshop expanded to the outdoors and to an art museum, I assessed their learning further. Some students described being outside as a new experience, even though they passed the area every day as their buses arrived or when they went out during recess. At the museum, students demonstrated their ability to respond to works of art and to discuss what they saw with their peers. They were able to approach paintings in a museum with authority, excitement, and enthusiasm. Maxine Greene (1978) writes, "If the humanities are indeed oriented to wide-awakeness, if dialogue and encounters are encouraged at every point, it might be possible to break through the artificial separations that make interdisciplinary study so difficult to achieve" (p. 165). When students pick up their clipboards, paper, and pencils and take them outside, to the neighborhoods, to museums, they have an opportunity to use the learning they have acquired in the classroom. Teachers constantly need to ask whether the work in their classrooms connects to the world.

In response to "The Art Teacher" Carl wrote, "My story as an artist, would probably be...when I was in kindergarten I loved to draw hills and trees. As I got older I liked to sketch and draw everything in art. Now I'm better at sketching and I'd like to keep going." I had followed Carl with interest throughout the year, drawing him at work, reading his artists notebook, questioning him, and talking with him. I was always surprised. For example, what I thought was a poem was actually a note to help him remember an image in his mind. Carl taught me about the importance of pace, the necessary mix of stretching one's margins, excelling, and playing in order to continue to create. By signing his name Carl van Gogh, he showed me what it meant to really believe in one's own work, to go beyond meeting someone else's standards of approval. Carl taught me about connections between the visual and verbal that led me to question and wonder about more possibilities. Robert Motherwell once said, "Each picture is only an approximation of what you want. That's the beauty of being an artist; you can never make the absolute statement, but the desire to do so as an approximation keeps you going." This energy was in Carl, too, who said, "I'd like to keep going." That is what will help me come to the last pages of this story, not to conclusions, but to further learning about the important role of observation, about bringing the arts into literacy.

We need to become wide awake to our own experiences as teachers, as learners, as children, to consider what aspects of our landscapes reside in the classroom, what pieces we bring to our classroom collages. In considering that, our classrooms need to reflect that landscape and become places where our stories inspire and propel our students' stories. Through that consciousness we can begin to name our expertise, identify our passions, and use them to enhance the learning in our classrooms. We can move away from presenting a curriculum toward putting life into the classroom.

We need to work toward making our classrooms workshops of learning—a literate community filled with opportunities for many ways of making meaning, surrounded with the works of artists, scientists, writers, and mathematicians, so that students can participate in apprenticeships of learning. As students begin to express themselves in many modes, it will be through our close observation that we can learn how they make connections with a work of art, a piece of literature, a poem, a song, or a dance. We need to observe our classrooms from outside and inside, to make our students our curricular informants.

When we as teachers and researchers begin to ask questions about student learning and our own practice, and take action on what we learn, our classrooms will become studios and laboratories of learning. We need to meet with teachers in our disciplines and others, on and beyond our grade levels, to share ideas, to help us begin to form whole pictures of learning, not just pieces divided into subjects, grades, and skills. When we begin to add portfolios and the information from our observations, interviews, and collections of student work, we can begin to understand how success in literacy is possible for more students through multiple ways of knowing.

We need to continue to tell stories of the learning we experience in our classrooms. On those first days in September, as I sat in the green chair recording how I felt about this new experience as the art teacher, noting what we did on each day and what I observed through my anxious vision, I was writing to help get through some difficult days. I thought then that one day this might be an interesting story. After all, I was an experienced teacher in a new situation and because of my ability to engage in deliberate and conscious learning, my story might be helpful to new teachers and to teachers in new situations.

Through writing I connected my own experiences as a teacher, artist, and child; I realized I was in the process of inventing a workshop based on many years of knowing.

That awareness made me rethink the way I so often referred to myself: "I'm just a teacher."

My story is not only for teachers of language arts who find themselves in an art classroom; it is a story for any teachers in a new situation who make meaning, who are conscious of what they bring to teaching and learning. My story is not about what to do, nor does it offer guidelines to make other classrooms look the same as mine. I hope to inspire others to reenvision their own classrooms with new eyes, through reading about the parallels and connections between writing and picturing that I saw, and to begin to make their own connections between movement and science, music and math, and more. My story, as Harold Rosen puts it, "only exists as a story by virtue of the existence of other stories" (p. 23). My story exists because of the stories of Ruth Hubbard and her work as a researcher in a first-grade classroom, examining the complementary processes of art and writing; Ralph Fletcher's clear voice describing his new experience of learning to teach teachers in New York City; and Nancie Atwell's stories of how her writing/reading workshop emerged as she learned with her students, helping us all realize that as classroom teachers we do more than just teach. Just as "The Art Teacher" inspired stories of learning from my students, I hope that my story will inspire other stories about learning in other classrooms. Too often, teachers turn to curriculum writers, coordinators, "experts," for answers when the teachers themselves have a wealth of answers that need to be tapped. I not only found more than just pictures in my artists workshop; I also became conscious that I had gained new understanding. I am no longer satisfied to say I am "just" a teacher.

During the last days of the artists workshop a second grader came over to watch me draw in my journal and commented, "You don't have a story or a picture about me." I quickly recorded her in my notes with a meandering line of my pen, feeling the urgency to capture all my students, and all of their stories, before the end of the school year. As

I wrote this book I knew that each piece was bigger than itself. What I wrote about one student or showed in one picture included many students, pictures, and words. In that way I know this is a story about all 365 students in my twenty-second year of teaching, just as I know that teachers' stories are more than just stories. Personal narratives are essential to our classroom practice, our continued learning, and our growth.

While last-day school activities went on upstairs in the "regular" classrooms, the "special" teachers had a chance to prepare for the summer vacation. I knew that the landscape of my classroom included the stories of my former students' learning, my passion and work as an emerging artist, my knowledge of teaching through observing my students over the years, and my childhood memories. Perhaps that is why I understood Jake when he responded to "The Art Teacher" by writing about his own history as an artist: "There are many happy moments in the following grades but none as important as when I was in kindergarten."

I took down the dangling signs and packed up the artists notebooks, the students' pictures, my journals, and the bulging folder marked "Here Miss Ernst, this is for you," which held the many gifts of pictures that students had spontaneously presented. Knowing some students might stop in unannounced, I printed one last message on the easel by the door. I hoped they would pass by and remember their work here. Everything I was taking with me reminded me of the ways my students' stories connected with my own. It all represented the learning—the demands, risks, and discoveries—we had experienced on our journey through the artists workshop.

Have a ♡ ♡
happy summer
Love, Miss Ernst

The end of the day on June 19, 1990 and I am
in the corner by the tape recorder—
listening to the interviews I
did today. The easel tells my
story... and it has been an
emotional day. I have taught

E*pilogue*

Two years later, as a result of increasing enrollment and several retirements, I was recalled to continue my work as the art teacher in the elementary school. It is there that I continue my inquiry, further examining questions about the artists workshop: What is the role of choice? How can writing be strengthened and expanded? What are further uses of the portfolio?

When I returned, my former kindergartners and first graders were third and fourth graders. Few remembered the orange snakes, but many remembered the dangling signs, their stories, their pictures. Their empowerment to learn and create has recharged both me and the workshop. It is there that I continue to learn, draw, write, and wonder with my young colleagues—all of us artists, writers, and learners.

References

Atwell, N. 1987a. Class-based writing research: Teacher learning from students. In *Reclaiming the classroom. Teacher research as an agency for change,* ed. D. Goswami and P. Stillman, 87–94. Portsmouth, NH: Boynton/Cook.

———. 1987b. *In the middle: Writing, reading, and learning with adolescents.* Portsmouth, NH: Boynton/Cook.

———, ed. 1990. *Coming to know: Writing to learn in the intermediate grades.* Portsmouth, NH: Heinemann.

Baylor, B. 1972. *When clay sings.* Illustrated by Tom Bahti. New York: Aladdin Books.

———. 1986. *I'm in charge of celebrations.* Illustrated by Peter Parnall. New York: Charles Scribner's Sons.

Bogdan, R., and S. Biklen. 1982. *Qualitative research for education: An introduction to theory and methods.* Boston: Allyn and Bacon.

Burnett, F. H. [1911] 1988. *The secret garden.* New York: Viking Kestral.

Calkins, L. M. 1986. *The art of teaching writing.* Portsmouth, NH: Heinemann.

dePaola, T. 1988. *The legend of the Indian paintbrush.* New York: G. P. Putnam's Sons.

———. 1989. *The Art Lesson*. New York: G. P. Putnam's Sons.

Dyson, A. H. 1990. Research currents: Diversity, social responsibility, and the story of literacy development. *Language Arts* 67:192–205.

Edens, C. 1980. *Caretakers of wonder*. La Jolla, CA: Green Tiger Press.

Fletcher, R. 1991. *Walking trees: Teaching teachers in the New York City schools*. Portsmouth, NH: Heinemann.

Gallas, K. 1991. Arts as epistemology: Enabling children to know what they know. *Harvard Educational Review* 61(1):40–50.

Gardner, H. 1991. *The unschooled mind: How children think and how schools should teach*. New York: Basic Books.

Glass, A. 1982. *Jackson makes his move*. New York: Frederick Warne.

Goennel, H. 1989. *Sometimes I like to be alone*. Boston: Little, Brown.

Graves, D. 1983. *Writing: Teachers and children at work*. Portsmouth, NH: Heinemann.

Greene, M. 1978. *Landscapes of learning*. New York: Teachers College Press.

———. 1988. *The dialectic of freedom*. New York: Teachers College Press.

———. 1991. Texts and margins. *Harvard Educational Review* 61(1):27–29.

Harste, J., and D. Rowe. 1986. Metalinguistic awareness in writing and reading: The young child as curricular informant. In *Metalinguistic awareness and beginning literacy: conceptualizing what it means to read and write*, ed. D. B. Yaden, Jr., and S. Templeton, 235–56. Portsmouth, NH: Heinemann.

Hubbard, R. 1989. *Authors of pictures, draughtsmen of words*. Portsmouth, NH: Heinemann.

———. 1991. Revisiting the world of children: Myths, metaphors, and new directions for research. *Teaching and Learning: The Journal of Natural Inquiry* 6:6–18.

John-Steiner, V. 1985. *Notebooks of the mind: Explorations of thinking.* New York: Harper and Row.

Lewis, C. S. 1950. *The lion, the witch, and the wardrobe.* New York: Macmillan.

Martin, R. 1989. *Will's mammoth.* Illustrated by Stephen Gammell. New York: G. P. Putnam's Sons.

Murray, D. M. 1982. *Learning by teaching: Selected articles on writing and teaching.* Portsmouth, NH: Boynton/Cook.

Nicolaides, K. 1941. *The natural way to draw.* Boston: Houghton Mifflin.

Rosen, H. 1985. *Stories and meanings.* Portsmouth, NH: Boynton/Cook.

Rylant, C. 1988. *All I see.* Illustrated by P. Catalinotto. New York: Orchard Books.

Samton, S. W. 1985. *The world from my window.* New York: Crown Publishers.

Walsh, E. S. 1989. *Mouse paint.* San Diego, CA: Harcourt Brace Jovanovich.

White, E. B. 1970. *The trumpet of the swan.* New York: Harper and Row.

Winner, E. 1982. *Invented worlds: The psychology of the arts.* Cambridge, MA: Harvard University Press.

Wiseman, A. 1975. *Making things. A handbook of creative discovery.* Book 2. Boston: Little Brown.

DATE DUE

OCT 25 '94	JU 5 '01		
	OC 23 '02		
MAR 19 '95	AG 30 '03		
APR 18 '95	MY 11 04		
MAY 17 '95	JE 22 '04		
NOV 8 '95	JY 08 '06		
FEB 27 '96	ILL		
	4/22/09		
ILL			
B733			
3/21/98			
AP 06 '99			
MAY 17 1999			
AP 06 00			
ILL			
6775790			
4/23/01			